MW01477744

TO EACH UNFOLDING LEAF

Selected Poems 1976-2015

PIERRE VOÉLIN

translated from the French by John Taylor

BITTER OLEANDER
PRESS

The Bitter Oleander Press
4983 Tall Oaks Drive
Fayetteville, New York 13066-9776
USA

www.bitteroleander.com
info@bitteroleander.com

Copyright © 2017 English translation, notes & introduction by John Taylor.

Copyright © 2017 by Pierre Voélin for the French poems included in the following books and sequences: *Les Bois calmés*, Éditions La Dogana, 1989; "Dans une prairie de fauche" (*Parole et famine*, Éditions Empreintes, 1995); *La Lumière et d'autres pas*, Éditions La Dogana, 1997; "Des cris et du silence" (*La Nuit accoutumée*, Éditions Zoé, 2002); "Le Poème en Arménie" (*L'Étrangère*, 40/41, 2017), "Y." (*The Fortnightly Review*, December 2015).

Copyright © 2016 by Éditions Fata Morgana for *Sur la mort brève*, *La Nuit osseuse*, *Lierres* and *Lents passages de l'ombre*.

Copyright © 2015 by Éditions La Dogana for *Des voix dans l'autre langue*.

Copyright © 2017 by Pierrette Demolon for the engraving "Planche de l'Almanach 2 / eau-forte et aquatint" by Pierre Tal-Coat.

Special thanks to the Swiss Arts Council *Pro Helvetia* for their support in making this translation project possible.

Grateful appreciation to Pierrette Demolon for her permission to have the engraving "Planche de l'Almanach 2 / eau-forte et aquatint" by Pierre Tal-Coat grace the cover of this collection of selected poems. With special thanks as well to the Galerie Hus in Paris and to the photographer Mario Camelo in Fribourg.

ISBN #: 978-0-9862049-6-8

Library of Congress Control Number: 2017932807
All rights reserved

No part of this book may be used or reproduced in any manner whatsoever without written permission from the translators and/or editor except in the case of brief quotations embodied in critical articles and reviews.

Layout & Design: Roderick Martinez

Manufactured in the United States of America

ACKNOWLEDGMENTS

Let me heartily thank the editors of the following publications, in which earlier versions of several poems by Pierre Voélin first appeared:

Modern and Contemporary Swiss Poetry, edited by Luzius Keller, Victoria, Texas / London / Dublin: Dalkey Archive Press, 2012: six poems from *In a Hay Meadow.*

The Bogman's Cannon (May 2015): eight poems from *Last Folds of the Promise.*

The Fortnightly Review (December 2015): the entire sequence *Y.*

Samgha (December 2015): eight poems from *The Calmed Woods.*

I am especially grateful to Paul B. Roth, the editor of *The Bitter Oleander,* for first publishing twelve poems from *In a Hay Meadow* in the Fall 2015 issue, and then for devoting a special feature to Pierre Voélin in the Spring 2017 issue, which includes an extensive interview and the sequence *Only Snow is Missing.*

TABLE OF CONTENTS

Introduction by John Taylor	ix
On Brief Death / Sur la mort brève (1984)	
On Brief Death	15
I. Whiter than Salt	17
II. Accompanied Speech	21
III. Late and Joyous	27
IV. A Shower of Raindrops	33
The Bony Night	37
The Calmed Woods / Les Bois calmés (1987)	51
Where the Apiaries are Closing	53
The Incurable	61
Night of November First	69
The Calmed Woods	81
Through the Heather	91
Of Screams and Silence / Des cris et du silence (1994)	107
from *Words and Famine / Parole et Famine* (1995)	
In a Hay Meadow / Dans une prairie de fauche	113
Light and Other Footsteps / La Lumière et d'autres pas (1997)	131
Downwind from Tsarmine Pass	133
Only Snow is Missing	149
In the Language of Ferns	167
The Poem in Armenia: Notes / Le Poème en Arménie: Notes (2009)	187
Y. / Y. (2015)	197
Voices in the Other Language / Des voix dans l'autre langue (2015)	227
A Squawking Sky	229
Voices in the Other Language	251
Last Folds of the Promise	291
Notes	311
Bibliography	321

INTRODUCTION

This book offers a representative selection of Pierre Voélin's poetry, ranging from his early books *Sur la mort brève* (On Brief Death, 1984) and *Les Bois calmés* (The Calmed Woods, 1987) to recent works such as *Y.* (Y., 2015) and *Des voix dans l'autre langue* (Voices in the Other Language, 2015). In other words, since *La Nuit osseuse* (The Bony Night) section of *On Brief Death* was written during the years 1976-1980, this *Selected Poems* spans four decades and reveals the Swiss poet's recurrent themes of amorous exaltation (and loss), an individual's relationship to nature (and especially to a rural environment), the possibilities of a spiritual quest in the contemporary world, as well as the writer's role (or vulnerability) with respect to political iniquity or persecution. Up to now, Voélin has remained very little known in English-speaking countries.

Yet he is one of the most important figures in contemporary Swiss francophone poetry. Born in 1949 in the village of Courgenay and then raised in the nearby small town of Porrentruy, both of which are located in the hilly Jura region of Switzerland, Voélin is a key poet in a generation that also comprises Frédéric Wanderlère (b. 1949), François Debluë (b. 1950), José-Flore Tappy (b. 1954), and Sylviane Dupuis (b. 1956). It is a generation that has sometimes chosen thematic directions differing from those taken by their Swiss mentors, namely Anne Perrier (b. 1922), Philippe Jaccottet (b. 1925) and Pierre Chappuis (b. 1930), and that has conceived new poetics to continue to question man's place in the cosmos.

This being said, it would be a serious error to read Voélin's poetry in an exclusively Swiss literary context. He was much more specifically influenced, as a young poet, by the poetry of René Char (1907-1988), Henri Michaux (1899-1984), and Francis Ponge (1899-1988), not to forget his student years at the University of Geneva, where Yves Bonnefoy (1923-2016) was one of his professors. Voélin has also cited his admiration for Jacques Dupin (1927-2012) and Jean Grosjean (1912-2006). The latter poet was especially enlightening to Voélin in his later search for the pertinence of Christian faith to the foundations of poetry and to our ways of representing the world.

Apropos of Voélin's own poetics, what strikes the reader coming for the first time to his verse is its lyricism. Within the context of French-language poetry from the second half of the twentieth century and to the present day, where prosodic concerns tend to be discreet or secondary, if not entirely absent, the poet's relative musicality stands out as something quite rare. Playing with assonance and occasional internal rhymes (much more than with end-line rhyming), especially arranging fragmentary phrases that have rhythmic, emotional, but not necessarily immediate semantic affinities, and suppressing all punctuation marks with the exception of dashes, Voélin has blown new life into the possibilities of French-language lyric poetry. But it must be specified that his particular conception of lyricism also favors suggestiveness, some but not all sources of effusion, and is modulated by a concern with authenticity and real corporal experience; his "music," which is no outright song, involves brief bursts of feeling as well as more subtle, subdued rhythmic movements. Ideally, the élan springs from the body, as it were, less from conscious thinking. In his series of short notes, "L'Oreille de Malchus" (Malchus's Ear) included in *La Nuit accoutumée* (The Customary Night, 2002), he cautions himself: "Be wary of the kind of lyricism that strips us bare—through its excess, its haughtiness, its pose, its posture, its vanity. Recall that lyricism is born in our humors, as ancient medicine would have put it: lymph, tears, blood, sperm."

The second notable feature of his work is how his poems, each of which is positioned in a thematically intelligible sequence, are often made up of fragmentary lines and sometimes oblique shifts in perspective. Such a style suggests at least two deep underlying ideas with philosophical ramifications. First of all, it is tempting to see in Voélin's style a perception of the disintegration of genuine speech, a disintegration at least partly consequential to the treacherous political discourse of the twentieth century or to contemporary modes of expression, and a simultaneous attempt to heal this wound, through poetry, by gathering up the bits and pieces into a coherent whole. Secondly, fragmentation for Voélin implies seeking the primordial image, or at least a proximity with the primary sense impression, however fleeting or incomplete, as the surest way of drawing out the essential emotions that come before thought; and the way he formulates these emotions that precede thought (or that spark memories or expectation) also naturally affect, indeed create, his subdued lyricism. As an example of the kind of primordial imagery that he seeks, "the swallows / . . . flying through the bannered wind / as you wove daisy stems through your hair" in this recent poem written in tribute to Anna Akhmatova (1899-1966):

> Yet for solitude—you carry off the sky
> your tears—cold snowy skies
>
> Yesterday—the swallows
> flying through the bannered wind
> as you wove daisy stems through your hair
>
> Days and nights tally up in their prison
> the marks traced by a child's finger
> are counted by fives...

This homage to Akhmatova is likewise typical. Voélin also pays tribute (several times) to Osip Mandelstam (1891-1938) and his wife Nadezhda (1899-1980), to Paul Celan (1920-1970), and to other poets who suffered from the evil of their times, as well as to two poets—Emily Dickinson (1830-1886) and Gerard Manley Hopkins (1844-1889) who, through their own use of fragmentation and primary imagery, have arguably been stylistic inspirations for him, especially in his later work, yet who are less immediately associated with the turmoil of history. Some of Voélin's poetry alludes to the death camps of the Shoah, an important element in his literary coming of age. His sensitivity to the extermination of the European Jews began with a visit, while he was a boy, to Dachau, in the company of his grandfather, who had helped the French resistance movement during the Second World War. The poet also alludes to the mass executions that took place during Stalin's reign in the Soviet Union, and, in more recent essays, to the genocide in Rwanda. His poetic prose piece "Screams and Silence" (1994) is addressed to the inhabitants of Sarajevo during the Yugoslav Wars (1991-1995, with subsequent battles through 2001). This text is included here because it also provides an essential statement of Voélin's poetics. He sometimes opens his poetry readings with this impressive text.

Yet on this specific level, Voélin's is no facile poetry of political commitment, no "protest poetry," but rather what one might call a "taking into account." While evoking the beauties of the Jura countryside, various rural labors (which he knows intimately, as several poems attest), his vanished childhood or the sensual flights of love, he by no means forgets the depravities of history: they must be taken into account. The Swiss critic and novelist David Collin sums up this aspect of Voélin's work thus: "He is one of the most important French-language poets of his generation. His oeuvre is at once exacting and humble, musical and grave, joyous and highly crafted. His poetry is like a response or a prelude to encounter, gesture, and listening. It questions the weight of words, the stakes of poetic language, the memory of twentieth-century persecutions, shame, and survival." A fine instance of what Collin expresses here is *Le Poème en Arménie* (The Poem in Armenia, 2009), a sequence of "notes" written in homage to Mandelstam (the author of *Voyage to Armenia*) and also relating Voélin's impressions during a trip taken to that country. The sequence includes some Christian symbolism, which appears in other poems as well. Such poetry, as the poet has himself explained, should be read in the context of the Catholicism of his native Jura region and not in that of the Protestantism of other parts of Switzerland. He has expressed his attachment to the "logos" of the Gospel of Saint John and the reader will notice allusions in some poems to the figure of Christ or the Virgin Mary. At least three other recurrent symbols—light, threshold, promise—at once relate to Christian themes and go beyond them in an attempt to accommodate an even broader vision of being, nature, and death.

He has called himself a "border poet," specifically referring to the proximity of his native region to the French border and, more generally, to his eagerness to cross borders, leave behind the confines of Switzerland, and deploy his European vision of contemporary life. The image can be extended literarily to his ways of departing from the framework of one theme (erotic attraction, for example) and crossing over into what seems to be a very different theme (the memory of mass execution). It is in this respect that, while he is inclined to fragmentary evocation, he seeks a wholeness of vision that encompasses the breadth of human experience.

I conceived this project of translating Voélin's work after rendering poetry by him and seventeen other Swiss francophone poets for the Dalkey Archive Press anthology, *Modern and Contemporary Swiss Poetry* (2012), and following upon my completion of similar representative selections of the poetry of Philippe Jaccottet, José-Flore Tappy, and Pierre Chappuis. As has already been suggested, one salient contrast, at least to Jaccottet's and Chappuis's poetics essentially oriented toward nature, is Voélin's way of assimilating his humanistic historical awareness into his crafted lyricism. In Chappuis's essay "Un baîllon poreux" [A Porous Gag Over the Mouth], published in *Tracés l'incertitude* (Outlines of Uncertainty, José Corti, 2003) and devoted to Voélin's work, the elder Swiss poet astutely notes:

> ... even worse and staining the [twentieth] century forever is the fate of millions of victims stripped of their humanity, sunk into horror and death through the will of other human beings. Poetry, as Voélin understands it, is nothing if, after Mandelstam, Celan and so many others, it does not ever bear within it, obscurely, even secretly, a part of this suffering, and if it does not at the same time tend to restore our human dignity to us, to "re-situate [us] in reality" by encompassing both what is best and what is worst, thus enabling us to accept at once 'the risk and the joy of living.'

Chappuis also points out that the "violence" inherent in Voélin's verse is "dictated by an élan of tenderness, a fraternal élan in which human beings and things are, or rather should be, embraced in a lyricism which is nonetheless reduced to mere fragments, even bits [of poetic speech], yet which is raised above those very consequences like river water splashing against its stony bed, a song caught up in this current that gets carried away yet only in order to play essentially with understatement." Chappuis's perception shows well how Voélin's poetry, which is composed of seemingly contradictory elements—violence and tenderness, fragmentation and wholeness—achieves a remarkable equilibrium.

As with all the French-language poets whom I have translated, my goal with Voélin's work has been to read as far as possible into the rich primary meanings, connotations, and allusions of the original, and bring them as exactly as possible into English. The nuanced lyrical quality of Voélin's French, not to mention his rejection (in much of his poetry) of punctuation and grammatical connectors, raise the additional challenge of creating an equivalent rhythmic élan in English which, at the same time, keeps its distance from traditional, formal rhythmic structures. My gratitude to Pierre Voélin! This translation could not have been carried out without his amiable and philologically precise answers to my many questions—by e-mail, by regular mail, and in two cafés in Paris, where we met in mid-February, 2016.

John Taylor
Saint-Barthélemy d'Anjou
January 1, 2017

TO EACH UNFOLDING LEAF

On Brief Death

Sur la mort brève

To the friend of wind and raindrops

À l'ami des gouttes et du vent

para que sobre lo quemado
caminemos sin miedo
en el aquí y ahora

so that on the ashes
we walk without fear
here and now

afin que sur les cendres
nous marchions sans peur
ici et maintenant

Homero Aridjis

I

Plus blanches que sel

La fleur du chemin, l'oubliée du feuillage, le myosotis poudreux de la douleur, toi, ce fut toi, et toi encore. Abandonnée, nue, sans la Comédie de la Soif. Sans que fût jamais perdu le battement sourd des heures.

Une chambre (si petite pour y mourir, disait l'aïeule) mais il n'est pas de chambre, seulement l'air à boire à pleins poumons. Sur la table du silence, le corps, renversé.
Le soleil – ses griffes n'y ont plus part.

Deux mains pour la prière aux agonisants ; deux autres qui veulent coudre tes paupières sur le secret. La mémoire glisse comme un lac de montagne. L'implacable mémoire.

Patience sur le lit de fièvres ! Ferveur de l'agonie. Buissons où le corps se consume ; les forceps, les longs cris, l'atroce. Telle, cette mue que l'on eût tant voulue simple et silencieuse. Épiée, guettée.
L'œil fixe de l'épervier au front du lit.

Sur le drap, en plus du visage, seules demeurent les deux mains lourdes, plus blanches que sel : quel ange va surgir pour les prendre dans les siennes, les reconnaître ?
Rumeur lointaine. Océan de lait. La chambre doucement bascule.

Contre les paumes du silence, enfin reposée, enfin la tête à l'abandon...

La toilette des morts – l'eau froide, le savon, la cuvette, la mentonnière et les doigts que l'on noue, tous les gestes accomplis, là – comme une tendresse ultime... et le vieux corps malade, à bout de forces... et la rive du temps qui s'efface.

I

Whiter Than Salt

The flower of the path, the forgotten one among the foliage, the dusty forget-me-not of pain, you, it was you, and you again. Abandoned, naked, without the Comedy of Thirst. Without the dull beating of the hours ever fading away.

A bedroom (so tiny to die in, the grandmother would say), but it's not a bedroom, only air to gulp down. On the table of silence, the body, sprawled out.
The sunlight—its claws no longer have a share in this body.

Two hands for the prayer to the dying; two others wishing to sew your eyelids shut over the secret. Memory glides like the surface of a mountain lake. Implacable memory.

Patience on the feverish bed! Fervor of the death pangs. Bushes where the body is burning up; forceps, long screams, atrociousness. So it was, this alteration we would so much have wished had been simple and silent. Spotted, awaited.
On the headboard, the sparrow hawk's steady stare.

On the bed sheet, besides the face, only the two heavy mains remain, whiter than salt: what angel will surge forth to take them into his, recognize them?
Remote murmur. Milky ocean. Slowly the bedroom totters.

Against the palms of silence, at last at rest, her head having at last let go . . .

Cleaning the corpse—the cold water, the soap, the washbowl, the chin strap and clasping the fingers together, all these actions carried out, now—like an ultimate tenderness. . . And the sick old body, overwhelmed. . . And the shore of time fading away.

Ses cheveux de payse, ses doigts si gourds, ses doux poignets bleuis — en terre, plantés. Touffes de sauge dans la combe du souvenir.
Mais le repos, le soir. L'os de sa face.

Bienheureuse solitude !
Sur la colline – en débris d'écorces, mottes, marne, cailloux, herbes et gerbes du tablier des morts.
Elle marche. On ne l'entend pas venir. Seules des feuilles récitent.

Au vieux Christ des carrefours, à ses mains de vigueur, l'eau bénite, l'eau lustrale, l'eau des pluies de résurrection.

À nouveau tinte sur le pré la petite cloche des morts ; la terre étouffe des sanglots. Tu te redresses. Au cœur la pesante argile du souvenir.

Péniblement elle marche dans le verger, appuyée à sa canne, beau bâton de pitié ; s'arrête ; souffle un peu ; se penche pour ramasser les fruits blets du poirier ; non, impossible de se courber... Il lui faudra attendre que vienne la petite fille, celle qui interroge la misère du regard tandis que les longues herbes sucrées, sous la jupe, émeuvent son sexe.

Tout tremble auprès de l'abreuvoir : le mince filet d'eau, le prunier et ces très vieux chevaux venus boire, leur robe claire soudain parcourue de tressaillements.
Fraîcheur – couleur aussi d'un dernier regard jeté sur la terre qui se referme comme un livre d'images.

Il n'est que d'apprendre les gestes, un à un. La survie, lente ou violente. Il y a ce cœur débourbé, si proche à nouveau du songe léger des chiens.

Et toute parole soit terre et lierres – terre pour son front, lierres humides à sa bouche. Contre absence, cette force. Deux mains saisissant l'échelle de bois blond. Naître et renaître.

PLUS BLANCHES QUE SEL

Her country girl's hair, her numb fingers, her soft wrists become blue—in the ground, planted. Tufts of sage in the mound of memory.
But a rest, in the evening. The bone of her face.

Blessed solitude!
On the hill—in debris of bark, dirt clods, marl, rocks, grass and sheaves from the apron of the dead.
She is walking. She cannot be heard coming. Only leaves are reciting.

To the old Christ of the crossroads, to His vigorous hands: holy water, lustral water, the rainwater of resurrection.

Again tolls over the meadow the little bell of the dead; the soil smothers the weeping. You straighten up. In your heart the weighty clay of memory.

She struggles to walk in the orchard, leaning on her cane, a fine stick of pity; stops; gets her breath back a little; stoops to pick up overripe fruit fallen from the pear tree; no, it's impossible to bend down... She'll have to wait for her granddaughter to arrive, who will ponder the miserable look in her eyes while the long sweet grass, beneath her skirt, stirs her sexual organs.

Everything is trembling near the watering trough: the thin trickle of water, the plum tree and these very old horses that have come to drink, their light-colored coats suddenly twitching.
Coolness—also the color of a last look cast onto the earth shutting like a picture book.

One only has to learn the hand movements, one by one. Survival, slow or violent. Here is a heart cleansed of its mud, once again so close to the weightless daydreaming of dogs.

And may every word be dirt and ivy—dirt for her forehead, moist ivy at her mouth. Against absence, this force. Two hands grasping the light-colored wood ladder. To be born and reborn.

II

La parole accompagnée

    Mais la honte aux commissures du temps !

    Le bois de hêtres. Les plaines à n'en plus finir. La poudre des os. Les plaies.
    Rien, cela, ce froid qui accompagnait toute parole.

    Et le voilà, vivant de peu, vivant de neige. Prié de se soumettre, le sachant. Pour que s'aiguisent encore ces débris de lames, de haches qui tournent au secret du cœur.
    Plus tard se partagera sa main aux écritures de pierre et de verre.

    Tout ce qui fut laissé pour boire ce peu de l'eau des pluies... pour habiter la face du silence.
    Dans l'épissure du dernier poème, l'exil infini de l'amour. Multiplié par les gouttes, l'effroi, le regard perdu.

    Qui sut toujours se tenir contre le ciel, la tête ouverte, gagnée lentement par l'éboulement des rocs.
    Tu échanges le visage où rêver. Ta bouche maintenant : le seigle âcre, la rosée, les flammes.

    L'autre face des pierres, ravivée. Tu la marques. À l'aise dans le vent nocturne. Ta mémoire ensanglante.
    Tu sauras te taire quand viendra l'obscur dénouement.

    Le visage blême, comme éclairé par l'unique douleur. La mort serre ses chevilles, empoigne. Mais lui, si simple, ses yeux sachant la reconduire dans le ciel, les arbres, le sentier.
    Il n'a pas fini de mâcher lentement le pain ! Bientôt, il soulèvera la lampe. Un geste... une pluie de miettes aux mésanges, petites nonnes aériennes célébrant la précarité du jour...

II

Accompanied Speech

      But shame at the commissures of time!

      The beech woods. The endless plains. The bone powder. The wounds.
      It was nothing, that chill accompanying every word.

      And here he is, living off little, living off snow. Ordered to obey, and knowing this. So that these debris of blades and axes turning in the secrecy of the heart will stay sharp.
      Later his hand will alternate between writing with stone and with glass.

      All that was left to drink, this little amount of rainwater... to dwell on the face of silence.
      In the splice of the last poem, the infinite exile of love. Increased by the raindrops, the horror, the empty stare.

      Who always knew how to stand up to the sky, his head split open, slowly overcome by the falling rocks.
      You exchange the face enabling you to dream. Your mouth now: the bitter rye, the dew, the flames.

      The other face of the stones, revived. You mark it. At ease in the night wind. Blood flows forth from your memory.
      You'll know how to stop speaking when the dark outcome occurs.

      The wan face, as if lit up by the single pain. Death grasps his ankles, grips them. But he, so simple, his eyes knowing how to lead death back into the sky, the trees, the path.
      He hasn't finished slowly chewing the bread! Soon, he'll lift the lamp... A movement of the hand... A shower of crumbs to the titmice, little aerial nuns celebrating the precariousness of the day...

Voilà qu'il revient poser la question de Dieu, de la lenteur de Dieu, de sa lenteur. Il montre ses poignets, son torse, ses jambes. Tant de brûlures !

Plus loin, chargées de suie et de neige, de longues barques remontent le fleuve.

Et que fut pour toi le gel des bouches entr'ouvertes, soudain pétrifiées ? Tu n'as pas voulu dormir mais précéder. Une respiration de roches. L'étincelant regard.

Desséché l'ongle du tyran.

Vainqueur.

N'ayant pas choisi de mourir. Qui te presse ? Te force à bénir ses adieux de février ?

Ils viennent, le dernier regard est pour la huche. Tout au long du voyage, l'odeur du pain lui sera promission.

Le froid pénètre la terre aimée (les baguettes des noisetiers, la pourriture des choux, l'amas des branches coupées, et plus avant, à l'écart, les tilleuls).

Combien de jours encore cette brûlure aux paupières ?

Et puis la nuit, dans l'entrebâillement des brumes, à la fenêtre, l'étoile qui fut propice. Elle est là, présente et courbe. Et tu voudrais la rejoindre ou la maudire infiniment avant que naisse le petit jour d'osselets blancs.

L'ancien bleu regard noyé de larmes et jaune – en miroir, un Christ de boutique... Coup de sangle dans l'hébétude matinale.

À ton visage, cette douleur... Le corps d'autrefois comme une histoire généreuse.

Lent retour du souvenir. Des pas furtifs croisent l'orvet des ruines, l'œil du jardin : sa défroque (peau morte, percée, rongée par les petites fourmis noires). Et le bâton enfantin, tout près. La table du sacrifice n'était qu'un lieu d'orties blanches.

Déjà l'innocence t'apprivoise.

Now he's coming back to raise the question of God, of God's slowness, of his own slowness. He shows his wrists, his chest, his legs. So many burns!

Farther on, long boats, loaded with soot and snow, head back up the river.

And what were the frosty, half-opened, suddenly petrified mouths for you? You didn't want to sleep, but rather go first. A boulder-like breathing. The dazzling gaze.

Withered, the tyrant's fingernail.

Vanquisher.

Not having chosen to die. Who is urging you? Forcing you to bless his February farewells?

They are coming, the last glance is for the bread bin. Throughout the journey, the fragrance of bread will be a promise.

The cold penetrates the beloved earth (the hazelnut switches, the rotting cabbages, the piles of pruned branches, and farther on, off to the side, the linden trees).

These burning eyelids for how many more days?

And then night, in the half-opened haze, at the window, the star that was favorable. There it is, present and curved. And you'd like to reach it or incessantly curse it before the white-knucklebone dawn is born.

The former blue gaze shrouded in tears and yellowish—mirroring a Christ trinket... A lash amid the morning stupor.

To your face, this pain... The bygone body like a generous story.

The memory slowly returns. Stealthy steps coming across the slowworm of the ruins, the garden's eye: its cast-off clothing (dead skin bitten into, gnawed at by little black ants). And the child's stick, nearby. The sacrifice table was merely a place covered by white dead-nettles.

Already innocence is taming you.

Titubant, proche d'autres compagnons que le feu dévisage... tu murmures, disent-ils...

(les reîtres, les cavaliers d'Apocalypse, jusqu'en leur folie d'éperons, leur rage, n'ont que des yeux de sable)

Lointaine, l'éternelle fiancée chasse d'une main les guêpes, serre sa bague farouche.

Staggering, near other companions whom the fire is staring down. . . you're murmuring, they say. . .
(the roughnecks, the Horsemen of the Apocalypse, even in their craze for spurs, their rage, have merely sandy eyes)

Far away, the eternal fiancée shoos away wasps with the back of her hand, clenches her fierce ring.

III

Tard et joyeuse

      La femme et le poète vivant dans la nuit de l'arbre, toutes les nuits de l'arbre ; au matin, vous repartiez comme ivres, et si légers.

    Ô barques de l'amour nocturne !
    Enfoncées dans la nappe étoilée,
    Brassez le ciel, forcez la route !

(celle qui demeure montre ses bras de lichen)

      La chair émue – et puis ces yeux qui s'ouvrent la nuit dans le mûrier de larmes.

      C'était la nuit de mai, avec ses grands papillons de soie grise et brune ; nous entrions du même pas dans la ville natale. Le vent fraîchissait contre nos fronts, contre nos dents.
      Tes yeux, la terre entière – soudain dételée, folle de ses bois, de ses vergers, de ses rivières. Un lourd cerceau d'enfant.
      Je te voyais sourire, boire à longs traits les heures liquides et noires – mais l'effroi grandissait de toucher au masque du poète...

      Il pleuvait. Leurs mains n'avaient pas su se joindre ; leurs yeux, immobiles, plus silencieux que la terre. Une suite de flaques noires. Comment demeurer face à face ? S'agenouiller dans la chambre, murmurer le pardon ?
      Disparaître, s'effacer... sur le lit, mussée, un peu de la paille humide du jour à tes doigts mêlée.
      À l'angle, sur la table, près du carreau sali, rêveur écorché, lui, qui se penche...

      De craie et de cendres ce haut jour que vous aviez bâti... et le rouge-gorge heurtait contre la vitre, ne se résignait pas. Quémandeur, savant et pur.
      Le vent parlait au vent.

III

Late and joyous

The woman and the poet living in the night of the tree, all the tree's nights; in the morning, you leave together as if drunk, and so lighthearted.

O boats of nocturnal love!
Sunk into the star-studded spread,
Stir up the sky, force your way through!

(she who stays behind shows her lichen arms)

The flesh is stirred—and then these eyes opening at night in the tearful blackberry bush.

It was the night of May, with its big silky gray and brown butterflies; we were striding into our hometown. The wind was ever chillier against our foreheads, against our teeth.
Your eyes, the entire earth—suddenly unharnessed, crazy about its woods, its orchards, its rivers. A child's heavy hoop.
I watched you smiling, gulping down the black liquid hours—but with growing dread to touch the poet's mask...

It was raining. Their hands hadn't known how to come together; their eyes, motionless, more silent than the earth. Black puddles in a row. How to remain face to face? Kneel in the bedroom, murmur forgiveness?
To vanish, to fade away... on the bed, nearly out of sight a little of today's moist straw mixed around your fingers.
At the corner of the table, near the dirty windowpane, he, the flayed dreamer, bending over...

Ashen and chalky this great day you two have built... and the robin was flying against the windowpane, stubbornly. A beggar, pure and learned.
The wind was speaking to the wind.

Un chant nouveau ne blanchirait plus sa mémoire. On savait qu'elle appelait celui dont l'amour lui manquait, le craintif ouvrier de la douleur ; elle continuait d'épeler sa couche, de suivre les coutures intimes... Oh ! son pas de fraîcheur ! son salut de prairie où pend le soleil !
Elle eut faim et soif de sa mort.

J'ai sauvé la cruche bleue où s'égouttait le rêve. J'en ai repris les morceaux à la boue. Cherchant. Devinant.
Chaque jour recommence l'éclat de ton sang !

Tard et joyeuse – debout – tu songes dans la nuit démembrée :
« J'aurai tenu la main d'Isis, la main de perce-neige... »

Sa parole est l'alouette, apparaissant, disparaissant.
Le ciel, le dos rêche des mottes lui sont preuve et refuge.

Celle qui recoud ses souliers dans les chambres, au crépuscule. Qui fait se détourner le bourreau, piétinant les larges foulards de sang.
Celle qu'on étrangle... desserrant le nœud coulant des nuits. La palpitation du secret.

Elle – toute absence aux pas de la colombe. Qui manque à la fontaine, encore et encore. Qui se dévoue, ayant renoncé les plaintes.
La douleur intacte, transmise.

Elle est venue occuper tout l'espace des neiges. Une éternité s'est ouverte.
Devant être celle qui achève. Se tient dans la stupeur ; abandonnée, droite.

Et toi, l'essuyeuse des sueurs, l'immobile lingère, ô compagne, nous rendras-tu un jour une nuit cette vie ? Et l'odeur du chèvrefeuille ? Et cette lampe pour aller sous les pluies ?
Nous marchons. La porte des bûchers est restée ouverte...

Elle va. Elle sait le moineau friquet, sa robe de bure, ses petits cris. Lui seul, continuant de porter dans son bec, pareil à une simple aiguille, tout l'avenir de la moisson.

A new song would no longer absolve her memory. We knew she was calling out to the man whose love she missed, the fearful worker of pain; she continued to spell out every syllable of his bed sheets, to follow every intimate hem. . . Oh! his refreshing footsteps! His greeting like a prairie with the sun hovering over it!
  She was hungry and thirsty for death.

  I saved the blue jug into which the dream was dripping. I recovered bits of it from the mud. Seeking. Guessing.
  Every day your blood brightens again!

  Late and joyous—standing—you muse in the dismembered night: "I'll have held the hand of Isis, the snowdrop hand. . ."

  His words are a lark, appearing, disappearing.
  The sky, the rough backs of the dirt clods, are proof and refuge for him.

  She who mends his shoes in the bedrooms, at dusk. Who makes the executioner turn away, trampling the large scarves of blood.
  She who is strangled. . . loosening the nightly nooses. The palpitating secret.

  She—oblivious to the dove's steps. Who is missing at the fountain, again and again. Who sacrifices herself, having renounced lamenting.
  The pain intact, handed on.

  She's come and filled out all the space of the snows. An eternity has opened up.
  Obliged to be she who finishes off. Standing in stupor; abandoned, upright.

  And you, wiping off the sweat, you, the motionless linen maid, O companion, will you give this life back to us one day one night? And the fragrance of the honeysuckle? And this lamp for going outside in the rain?
  We are walking. The door to the pyres has remained open. . .

  She is going. She has known the tree sparrow, its homespun dress, its little chirps. All by itself continuing to carry in its beak, like a simple needle, all the future of the harvest.

Ne plus savoir vivre et naître que d'ombre et dans l'ombre servir. Les yeux sont pris sous le gel.

Les mains s'ouvrent et se ferment, déplacent les bols, un plus haut silence.

No longer knowing how to live and be born except from shadow and in the shadow to serve. The eyes are frozen beneath the frost.

The hands are opening and closing, moving the bowls, a higher silence...

IV

Une pluie de gouttes

      La verte infortune, dévisagée. J'ai dit la mort, dégrafé sa chaleur – poussières vaines de l'azur, terrain de sel, haie vive des secrets, grains, granit du royaume.
      Fontaines aux paroles.

      J'aime que tu sois l'homme s'arrachant des larmes, dehors, sous un dais de moustiques. Ta bouche réclame de l'air et de l'air. Qu'ils attachent tes mains, qu'ils enfoncent leurs poings dans ta joue, qu'ils murent tes yeux ?
      Tour à tour, le milan, la taupe, les biches redessinent la trace. Ô soins de pauvreté !

      Pour te voir, il manque l'air et la source ; il manque un commencement de feu. Et ces blessures aux alouettes – ce pur amour aveugle à vivre.

      Ramène à toi la barge du silence, ô prophète, qui vit dans l'espérance et le dégoût des jours. Dire pourquoi je m'achemine dans le fracas des rues m'est impossible.

      Tout est là. Entre parole et vanité de parole. Comme un secret, une vitre brisée où s'abat l'hirondelle. Tête tranchée, bouche heureuse.
      Es-tu celui qui patiente ? Des promenades sur des fleuves t'ont distrait. Il n'y a pas de mélancolie – seulement ton regard étonné, tes mains vides, une vague maison de buée au carreau...

      Noter ce qui s'accomplit dans l'oubli – sang des coqs sur les calcaires blancs du pays ; telles germinations, telles flagellations de ronces ; les pierres, nombreuses, éclatées ; cette brassée de bois d'enfance. Ô cendres et cendres des anciens feux !
      S'en aller heurter de la tête le soc du temps.

IV

A Shower of Raindrops

    Sharp green misfortune, stared down. I've told of death, unhooked its warmth—futile dust motes of the azure, salty land, hedge vibrant with secrets, seeds, granite of the realm.
    Fountains of words.

    I'm pleased you're the man ripping your tears out, outside, beneath a canopy of mosquitoes. Your mouth is begging for air and more air. May they bind your hands, smash their fists into your cheeks, wall up your eyes.
    In turn, the kite, the mole, the does retrace the tracks. O the cares of poverty!

    There's no air, no source, making you visible; there's no kindling of a fire. And these larks deviously wounded—this pure blind love to endure.

    Bring back that barge of silence to yourself, O prophet, you who live in the hope and the disgust of the days. To say why I move forward amid the roar of the streets is impossible.

    Everything is there. Between words and the vanity of words. Like a secret, a shattered windowpane against which a swallow smashes. Head severed, mouth pleased.
    Are you the one waiting? Outings on the rivers have amused you. There is no melancholy—only your astonished look, your empty hands, a vague misty house on the windowpane...

    Noting what is accomplished in oblivion—rooster blood on the white limestone of the land; certain germinations, certain flagellations of brambles; the many shattered stones; this armful of childhood wood. O ashes and ashes of former fires!
    Going away and striking one's head against the plowshare of time.

Qui insultera l'étoile ? Qui ruinera le soleil ? Écroulera les chemins des lunes ?

La plaie rouvre de l'enfance offerte au bourreau.

Les fourmis noires, la peur. En procession sur les feuilles mortes. Leur tâche dans la gloire du hêtre défait. Ébruiteuses d'éternité.

Contre l'extrême bord du ciel. Elles accumulent.

Par la manche du soleil. Par le rayon des paroles, malgré le sang.

Des mains timides s'obstinent et durent, tisserandes, jusqu'à l'achèvement du supplice.

Arrêtoir de la nuit.

J'arrache l'herbe des nuées. Cascade, lapidation de rires frais. Te les jette au visage, éternel crucifié.

Mendiant, il est fou que je revienne, à grands pas, par les vergers. Que je revienne attabler le mensonge.

Toi, dans la profusion des herbes, si lent à franchir les seuils dans l'air. Avance. Un pas, puis l'autre pas. N'ayant qu'une parole qui efface, qui resplendit.

Le siècle à genoux.

Tu n'es même plus l'homme qui s'avance, éreinté, incrédule, sans fièvre, sans pardon ; impossible d'habiter la langue vierge, d'être le confesseur ébloui du visible...

L'agneau futur est pendu dans la hêtraie. Le songe et le sang – goutte à goutte – sur les fougères.

Et ce n'est qu'une pluie de gouttes, fraîches ou sombres, une pluie de gouttes lentes, qui tremblent et ferment des yeux trop longs à guérir.

À Barberêche, automne 1982-printemps 1983

Who will insult the star? Who will ruin the sun? Tear down the paths of the moons?

The wound of childhood offered up to the executioner is opening again.

Black ants, fear. In procession over the dead leaves. Their chores in the glory of the ravaged beech. Newsmongers of eternity.

Against the farthest edge of the sky. They accumulate.

Through the sunlight's sleeve. Through the sunray of words, despite the blood.

Shy weaver's hands keep on working and last until the torture has been accomplished.

Stop-valve of the night.

I rip grass from the clouds. Waterfall, fresh laughter like hurled stones. I throw them at your face, eternal crucified Christ.

Beggar that I am, it's crazy for me to stride back through the orchards. To stride back to make the lie take its seat at the table.

You, amid the abundant grass, how slowly you cross the thresholds in the air. Move forward. One step, then another. Having only one word that effaces, that gleams.

The century on its knees.

You're no longer even the man moving forward, exhausted, incredulous, without fever, without being forgiven; it's impossible to dwell in the virgin language, to be the dazzled confessor of the visible. . .

The future sheep is hanging in the beech grove. The dream and the blood—drop by drop—on the ferns.

And it's merely a shower of raindrops, cool or dark, a shower of slow trembling raindrops that close eyes taking too long to heal.

In Barberêche, Autumn 1982-Spring 1983

The Bony Night

La Nuit osseuse

Tomorrow give me back my daylight emptied of days

Redonne-moi demain mon jour vidé de jours

—Pierre Jean Jouve, *La Vierge de Paris*

C'était famine
J'avais tes yeux tremblant pour la sagesse

Mais plus proche
de qui trempe sa lèvre à la coupe du froid

Et rien que le silence – ses doigts sévères
où se tisse et se défait le cœur –

L'errante offre sa tête au carrefour
il faut partir

S'en aller – d'un feu à un autre feu
La forêt n'a pas lieu dans les larmes

Ta louange va aux sueurs bleues de l'été
à des haies à des chemins

Ailleurs les pas d'un enfant distrait
font trembler le cimetière allemand

Elle prononce l'absence
quand je veux l'eau et la main de l'enfant

mémoire à ces lèvres qu'un vol de cailloux blancs

LA NUIT OSSEUSE

There was famine
I had your eyes trembling for wisdom

But closer
to whoever sips from the bowl of the cold

And nothing but silence—its severe fingers
where the heart is woven and unraveled—

The wandering woman offers her head to the crossroads
it's time to leave

To go away—from one fire to the next
The forest doesn't take place within tears

Your praise goes to the blue sweat of summer
to hedges to paths

Elsewhere an absentminded child's footsteps
make the German Cemetery tremble

She pronounces absence
when I want the water and the child's hand

memory to these lips a toss of white pebbles

J'ai rebâti l'ossuaire de la parole

Si léger est le corps amoureux
– territoire de flammes et de raisin

Ai-je sacré l'espace
mes mains dans ses mains de sel

Ai-je su deviner ses larmes
mes veines envahies par le feuillage

Et cette langue contournée
debout dans le chêne
l'ai-je parlée noueuse et secrète

et si longtemps perdue

Sur l'herbe des nuées un soc de lumière

Je sais l'âme en partage
à des berges noires au gravier d'eau
à l'étoile plus silencieuse de l'étang

I've rebuilt the ossuary of speech

So light is the loving body
—territory of grapes and flames

Have I consecrated space
my hands in her hands of salt

Have I known how to make out her tears
my veins invaded by foliage

And this contorted language
risen inside the oak
have I spoken it as knotty and secret

long lost

On the grass of the clouds a plowshare of light

I know the soul is shared out
to black embankments to the gravelly streambed
to the more silent star of the pond

Il n'est que de marcher aveugle
quitter la nuit osseuse

L'esprit s'ouvre à des puits de neige

Des voix disent que des mains saignent

À nouveau l'épée le murmure

Ô vous reprises à des champs de pierres
à de profonds sommeils d'herbe
aux feux multiples
à la suie aux rocailles

Sentinelles obscures

Quelles voix vous rappellent
quels murmures vous gouvernent
sous la couronne du hêtre défait

There's nothing left but to march blindly
leave the bony night behind

The mind opens to snow-filled wells

Voices say hands are bleeding

The sword again murmurs this

O you women taken back from stony fields
from the deep sleep of the grass
from the countless fires
from the soot from the rocky ground

Dark sentinels

What voices call you back
what murmurs rule you
beneath the crown of the ravaged beech

Ô délivrée
que retient l'ombre sûre de l'oiseau

pleureuse printanière

Et plus simple
qu'un enfant joueur sur les dalles du soir

tes bras ton offrande
deux étaux de lumière

Par d'autres voix d'enfant surprise
affolée

Celle qui meurt alourdie suppliante
– un bâillon de seigle sur la bouche

D'anciennes fêtes rouvrant leur manteau
et la miséricorde en pleurs

O freed woman
held back by the bird's sure shadow

spring weeper

And simpler
than a child playing on the flagstones of evening

your arms your offering
two vises of light

By other children's voices she's surprised
panicked

She who dies burdened imploring
—a gag of rye over her mouth

Ancient feasts opening their coats again
and mercy weeping

Et les vents soient de silex
un seul feu défroisse les forêts

Que toute bête s'en aille aux lisières

Disparaissent ses yeux sa langue
pourrisse sa tête improbable

Sur la fleuve que visitent les barques du deuil

le sommeil s'est épris du sommeil

La terre a muré la bouche des morts
plus bas est à l'œuvre la lumière
– tisserande du long sommeil

Je sais aggraver le silence

And may the winds be of flint
a single fire smooth out the forests

every animal flee to the edges

Her eyes her tongue vanish
her improbable head rot away

On the river visited by boats of mourning

sleep is smitten by sleep

The earth has walled over the mouths of the dead
the light is at work farther down
—weaver of the long sleep

I know how to deepen silence

Se taire et mourir aux visages
un à un disparus

Je suis quitte — tant de regards m'épargnent

Février jette sur la neige une poignée d'abeilles

Femme — et la mélodie sobre des fougères
voyageuse votive souffrante
ayant su le sang —

Je reconnais cette langue
où glisse un amas d'étoiles pauvres

Nous partageons la saveur de la terre
portons le jour contre le jour

1976-1980

To stop speaking and die for the faces
vanished one by one

I've paid up—so many looks spare me

February tosses a fistful of bees onto the snow

Woman—and the sober melody of the ferns
suffering votive voyager
having known blood—

I recognize this language
over which a cluster of poor stars slide

We share the flavor of the earth
carry the daylight against the daylight

1976-1980

The Calmed Woods

Les Bois calmés

One builds only the fault.
The victory is the dilapidation.

On ne construit que la faute.
La victoire est délabrement.

Pierre-Albert Jourdan

Où se ferment les ruchers

Les plaies d'Orion s'enveniment
Nous n'en finissons plus de souffrir

L'homme double s'est épris de sa fatigue

Il ne taillera plus le roseau des syllabes
il ne nous couvrira plus de sa pitié

Ton escorte les branches qui saignent
ta soif une eau de cruche

Vain est l'appel des juments
– leurs fers sont gravés sur ta gorge

Plus tendres d'autres yeux te suivent
leurs cils mêlés à la nuit

Mais le pelage que fouille doucement le souffle

À peine achevées – nuques brisées
les bêtes recommencent un autre silence

Where the Apiaries are Closing

Orion's wounds are festering
We're not at the end of our pains

Dual man is smitten with his weariness

No longer will he whittle the reed of syllables
no longer will he cover us with his pity

For your escort the bleeding branches
for your thirst water from a jug

Mares appealing in vain
—their horseshoes etched on your throat

You're followed by more tender eyes
their eyelashes blended with the night

But that fur a breath of wind softly ruffles

As soon as they are finished off—their necks broken
the animals again begin another silence

Par quelle porte évadée la langue de l'essaim
par quelle sente de pierres vives
quel secret jamais tu

Nous t'avons connue avec le bruit de l'eau
avec les hampes du lierre
sœur pauvre
arrachée aux épines
prise et reprise aux marches du sommeil

J'ai confié sa tête à la chute des météores
ses doigts aux jouets du vent

Une dernière fois le sang jaillit sous l'écorce
Ô printemps – frère sans égal
appuyé sur le silence et sa neuve éclisse

Sagement nous voulons bénir la vie
Tirant sur les vergues de sable
les constellations remontent dans nos mains

Des bêtes viennent souffler aux lisières
des passereaux saignés par la lumière

Même le silence n'a pas su nous délivrer

Through which door has fled the language of the swarm
over which path of living stones
which secret never left untold

We came to know you with the water's noise
with the leafy stalks of ivy
needy sister
torn from the thorns
taken and taken again from the steps of sleep

I've entrusted his head to falling meteors
his fingers to playthings of the wind

One last time blood is gushing beneath the bark
O spring—unequaled brother
leaning on silence and his new violin rib

We wisely wish to bless life
attaching sails to the spars of sand
the constellations rise again into our hands

Animals near the edges of woods to breathe
and passerines bled by the light

Even silence didn't know how to free us

Tes yeux en allés sur cette crête
fouillant les boqueteaux
buvant à longs traits le ciel
s'étourdissant d'oiseaux

Mépris du veilleur qui brûle ses fagots
son bâton ruine l'oronge et sabre l'ancolie

Tu n'aimes que la bure des fossés
vers toi rampent les sentiers à peau de fouine

Quelle rage éteint le souffle des forêts
Le long d'un arbre aux genoux moisis
circulent les grimpereaux

Nulle parole n'abrite cette fin du jour
Pas de traces sauf l'orchis et le vent
le doux balancement des fougères

Et je m'en vais saluer d'anciens prêtres muets
si étonnés d'avoir accompagné la vie

Le silence remue ses copeaux clairs
sans exaucer le cœur

un seul regard suffit à notre étreinte

OÙ SE FERMENT LES RUCHERS

Your eyes are gazing over this ridge
groping in the copses
gulping down the sky
getting drunk on birds

Scorn of the watchman burning his firewood
his stick smashing the agaric and slashing the columbine

You love only the dirt-brown homespun of the ditches
the marten-skin trails are crawling towards you

What rage snuffs the breath of the forests
The treecreepers fluttering
Up and down the moldy knees of a tree

No word shelters this end of day
No traces save the orchis and the wind
the soft swaying of the ferns

And off I go to greet speechless ex-priests
so astonished to have accompanied life

Silence is stirring its light-colored wood shavings
without granting the heart its wish

a single glance suffices for our embrace

Visage sous le masque – tombe de calcaire
où vient battre la lumière criblée

L'amour impur te cherche dans les ruines

Homme aux pouces de granit
au crâne recousu

glissant sous la hanche des saisons
le mensonge infini

riant et dressant tes tréteaux

Homme bu par la mort
sans l'ombre ni les roses
sans plus la force de combattre

Face behind the mask—limestone tomb
against which beats the filtered light

Impure love is looking for you in the ruins

Granite-thumbed man
with his sewn-up head

slipping the infinite lie
beneath the hip of the seasons

laughing and setting up your trestle table

A man drunk down by death
with neither shade nor roses
nor any energy left with which to fight

L'inguérissable

La nuit reprendre cette marche à la pourriture
longuement goûter les saveurs de la boue

Le temps – son crâne à découvert
et le tournoiement de poussières invisibles

Terre – ô terre venue justifier l'amas des corps

Rien ni personne qui puisse effacer les jours
leur noire et silencieuse calligraphie
leurs doigts écorcés

Céphée – son pouvoir de suie
à l'instant où se ferment nos paupières

notre solitude est prise à la rumeur des herbages

Disloquées – si accueillantes aux pluies
les barges qui s'enfoncent
Contre les pommiers elles piègent le silence

Deux mains suffisent
à clouer les ailes ouvertes d'une effraie

Enfants
penchez-vous sur la mare où bascule le ciel
écoutez le galop des pouliches et des ombres

The Incurable

Take back up at night this march to rottenness
taste at length the flavors of the mud

Time—its skull exposed
and the whirling invisible motes of dust

Earth—O earth here to justify this heap of bodies

Neither anything nor anyone can erase the days
their black silent calligraphy
their peeled fingers

Cepheus—his sooty power
just when our eyelids are shutting

our solitude is taken from the murmur in the pastures

Falling apart— so welcoming to the rains
the barges sink
Against the apple trees and entrap silence

Two hands suffice
to nail down a barn owl's spread wings

Children
bend over the pond where the sky is tottering
and listen to the gallop of fillies and shadows

Avec les branches du bois flotté
s'en vient l'étoile – sa triple amertume

Au loin une jeune fille s'étonnait la nuit
récitant ses prières
brodant sans fin ses robes d'anémones

Où étaient ses frères et ses sœurs

Incertaines vont les barques
nous ne voyons pas s'effondrer les berges

Laissez-le s'en aller
s'éloigner derrière la vitre bleue du vin

Ses bras ne vont plus charger la paille
trop de nuits l'abandonnent

Laissez-lui l'écorce le simple jeu des ombres
à sa bouche
plaquez les feuilles d'érable sycomore

Laissez-lui la cohorte des bêtes frileuses
et celles qui trébuchent
et seulement le cri des bêtes prises

With branches of driftwood
came the star—its triple bitterness

In the distance a girl was astonished
reciting her prayers at night
endlessly embroidering her anemone dresses

Where were her brothers and sisters

The unsure rowboats move onward
we don't notice the riverbanks caving in

Let him leave
move off behind the wine's blue pane

No longer will his arms load the straw
too many nights abandon him

Leave him the bark the simple interplay of shadows
on his mouth
press down the sycamore-maple leaves

Leave him the cohort of shivering animals
and those that stumble
and only the squealing of those caught

THE INCURABLE

Tu ne sais plus la langue de la douleur
traversant le bois de hêtres
ces terres où s'entassaient les corps

Naît une ruche qui te mitraille d'abeilles
naissent des alouettes grises

Tu questionnes au front l'étoile naine

Avec ou sans le froissement de la lumière
tu viens tu déblaies la bouche des martyrs

parole qui a souvenir du plus haut silence
parente des fétuques et des rouvres
des tas de pierres bises

Celle qui précède

   Le nom confié au silence, à la pourriture des souches, au lieu secret des lichens.
   Dans la mémoire atroce, recomposer les gestes d'Antigone, avec les ongles raclant la terre, rassemblant les poignées de terre, insultant, bénissant le vent.

Des femmes prient – gardiennes du souvenir
tandis que la mort occupe les bois légers

Des gouttes s'allument sous leur porte en fer
où sont prisonniers les regards et les mots

Une voix une seule appelle les pluies

No longer do you know the language of pain
as you cross through the beech woods
these lands where heaps of bodies rise

A hive is born and riddles you with bees
gray larks are born

You question the forehead of the dwarf star

With or without the rustling of the light
you're coming you're clearing out the martyrs' mouths

words that remember the highest silence
relatives of the fescue grasses and the sessile oaks
and the heaps of grayish-brown rocks

She who goes first

      The name entrusted to silence, to rotting stumps, to the secret spot where lichens grow.
      In atrocious memory, recompose Antigone's gestures, her fingernails scratching the earth, grasping fistfuls of earth, cursing, blessing the wind.

Women praying—guardians of the memory
while death dwells in the light woods

Drops flickering up beneath their iron door
where looks and words are prisoners

One and only one voice calls out to the rains

THE INCURABLE

à M., la plus vive enfant

Un souffle et le fracas du verre brisé
une pluie de sang

Parfums – paupières qui se referment

Ta mère épelle un nom dans la paroi de glace
un nom d'archange que mure déjà le crépuscule

Plus tard viendront les larmes
et cette lenteur arrachée à trop de gerbes
cette lenteur jusqu'à l'épuisement des jours

Les pensées par le froid – têtes bleues
abandonnées aux rêves de neige

Comme pour convoquer les traces
autour de l'inguérissable
l'azur en lambeaux

L'homme serre sa blessure méditant
dans la tour de rumeurs
à l'étroit l'hiver

to M., the liveliest child

A mere breath of wind and the crash of shattered glass
blood raining down

Fragrances—eyelids shutting

Your mother is spelling out a name into the wall of ice
an archangel's name already walled in by twilight

Later tears will come
and this slowness torn from too many sprays of flowers
this slowness until the days have run out

Thinking through the cold—bluish heads
left to dreams of snow

As if to summon the traces
around the incurable
the azure in shreds

The man grips his wound meditating
in his tower of murmurs
where he's cramped in winter

Nuit du premier novembre

à la mémoire de Paul Celan

nunc dimittis...

À l'herbe s'en va l'étoile
et sur la rive le poète se tient muet

C'en est fini des chemins de traverse
Curieuse à ses chevilles la terre
se rafraîchit

Il rouvre encore les pages noires de l'ortie
avant que d'un coup ne l'embarque un fleuve

Faucheur épié par l'œil des ténèbres
tu hais ta soif
tu réclames ta part à la douleur

Tu t'agrippes
lentement tes mains se nouent à l'épine blanche

Pour nous ton pain est retourné
ton vin désigne le bourreau

Night of November First

to the memory of Paul Celan

nunc dimittis...

Off goes the star to the grass
and the poet on the bank stands speechless

No more shortcuts are left
The curious earth is cooling
at his ankles

Once again he opens the black pages of the nettle
before a river suddenly sweeps him away

Reaper spied on by the eye of darkness
you hate your thirst
you claim your share from pain

You cling
slowly your hands clutch the hawthorn

For us your bread is upside down
your wine points to the executioner

Fiancée de la mémoire – ô reine d'incertitude
Que tes lèvres se déplient sous l'écorce
qu'une lame vienne ouvrir tes veines
que saigne enfin ta bouche

J'ai laissé des faînes dans tes poings

Tu n'es que le vent et la langue défaite
avec ce peu d'ombre qui bouge à tes côtés

Avec leurs yeux plissés de guérisseur
les hêtres me font signe

Partout la chevêche s'arme pour mourir

Jaunes les blessures que l'air visite
Bientôt se relève la troupe des bûcherons

Derrière eux le fer les branches le verre pilé
la parole que n'émiette pas le pain

Cette nuit par grâce le silence est la demeure
une main veut rajuster la nappe des eaux
– quelle faim d'étoiles

Tu hésites à franchir le pont
ton épaule se creuse pour des larmes

Tu t'étonnes de la proximité d'un visage

NUIT DU PREMIER NOVEMBRE

Fiancée of memory—O queen of uncertainty
May your lips unfold beneath the bark
may a blade open your veins
may your mouth bleed at last

I've left beechnuts in your fists

You're but wind and language come undone
with this slight shadow shifting at your sides

With their eyes squinting like a healer's
the beech trees are beckoning to me

Everywhere the little owl equips itself to die

Yellow are the wounds visited by the air
Soon the troop of woodcutters will rise

Behind them the iron the branches the crushed glass
the words left uncrumbled by the bread

Thankfully tonight the dwelling place is silence
a hand seeks to adjust the tablecloth of the waters
—what a craving for stars

You hesitate to cross the bridge
your shoulder makes a hollow for tears

You're surprised how close one face is

Être là – seul dans les poignantes ruines
Surtout ne pas toucher aux lèvres du ciel

Nous sont comme sœurs les colombes
Elles vont et viennent et boitent
sur leurs pattes rongées

Pour nous arracher au jeu des consolations
vite – qu'on les appelle et qu'elles se nomment

Les morts – nous les écoutons impassibles
Arceaux de la douleur toile du souvenir
et dessous tant de bouches qui halètent

qui veulent crier – oh presque nuls
entre l'absence et les tombes
les noms juifs de la terre
les colonnes creuses de cette terre

Being there—alone among the poignant ruins
Above all leave untouched the lips of the sky

The doves are like sisters to us
Coming and going and limping
on their gnawed feet

To tear us away from consolation games
quick—let's call out to them and have them say their names

The dead—we listen to them impassively
Archways of pain tissue of memory
and so many panting mouths underneath

wanting to cry out—Oh almost mere nothings
between absence and the graves
are the Jewish names of the earth
the hollow columns of this earth

NIGHT OF NOVEMBER FIRST

Nuit du premier novembre

I

T'éloignant tu cèdes la liste des noms perdus
Mères d'autrefois bercées par les bouquets
mêlées aux écluses aux roues des moulins

Paris sous ton pas – ses chandails de goudron
rien qu'un pont jeté vers la lumière

Une feuille de l'acacia vient de trembler
tu lui réserves les murmures

Et les yeux des statues voyagent dans l'airain

II

Pour toi l'œil ouvre l'œil des morts

et ne pas s'endormir avec la douleur
ni chasser nos chiens sous la paupière d'Orion

Vois – le bois du deuil se disloque

Qu'il flotte et s'en aille au fil des eaux
jusqu'à heurter le barrage et l'étoile

Night of November First

I

Moving off you give away the list of lost names
Mothers from yesteryear cradled by bouquets
and blended with canal locks wheels of watermills

Paris underfoot—its sweaters of tar
a mere bridge tossed over to the light

An acacia leaf has just quivered
you're saving murmurs for it

And the statues' eyes are moving within the bronze

II

For you the eye opens the eye of the dead

and keep from falling asleep with the pain
and from hunting our dogs beneath Orion's eyelid

Look—the grieving driftwood is coming apart

May it float away down the current
until it strikes the dam and the star

Alors s'élancera la voûte de ses cris
alors s'ouvrira son visage

Nous savons qu'il marchait sur la terre feue
qu'il saluait en passant les faucons

Maintenant les nuits prennent fin
nous sommes sans paroles

Il y a ces doigts que serre l'eau gelée

Seuls à deux pas du gouffre – toi et moi
accomplissant le vœu de la bruyère

Toi seul à l'abri – quel biseau retaille tes orbites

Les jours qui aiment à se tenir immobiles
les jours sur leurs talons calcinés

Je me penche pour cueillir l'herbe guérisseuse

Pas de place aux oracles

Au ciel claque le linge de l'orage
Nous pressentons les désastres

NUIT DU PREMIER NOVEMBRE

Then his cries will rush up like a lofty vault
then his face will open

We know he walked on the dead earth
greeted the falcons in passing

Now the nights are coming to an end
we are left wordless

And here are these fingers gripped by the frozen water

Alone two steps from the abyss—you and I
carrying out the heather's vow

You alone are sheltered—what bevel recarves the orbits of your eyes

The days that love to stand still
the days on their charred heels

I bend down to pick the healing herb

No room for oracles

The storm's linen flaps against the heavens
We have a foreboding of disasters

Muré dans quelle solitude
j'écoute les mots tourner dans sa bouche
pont d'argile et neiges orphelines

Le frêne d'une luge s'enflamme dans ses yeux
– pour la conservation du silence

Les rêves tous les rêves sont de communion

Walled up in such solitude
I listen to the words turning in his mouth
clay bridge and orphan snows

The ashwood slats of a sled blaze up in his eyes
—for the preservation of silence

Dreams all dreams are of communion

Les Bois Calmés

           pour Pierre Chappuis, dans l'inquiétude de la poésie

Quel miel amer coule à nos lèvres
quels vols de ronces traversent nos yeux

Attache des frelons – notre secours

Aveugle sous la taie blanche du pèlerin
son aile t'appartient

Ensemble nous mesurons des arpents de friches
nous portons la lenteur dans le feuillage

C'est ici notre alliance scellée par la ruse

Douleur est l'autre voix qui nous rassemble
M'accompagne la main de ronces

errante sur les jardins aux perches grises
crevant la toile des puits

Elle étonne elle passe familière

Des mots qu'il reste une poussière de roseau
un tissu de cendres ou ces coupures
ce liseré de sang à ta main

Tu viendras tu porteras le joug du feuillage
ton pas gagné à la douleur

The Calmed Woods

> for Pierre Chappuis, in the disquiet of poetry

What bitter honey flows at our lips
what flights of brambles cross our eyes

Attach the wasps—our salvation

Blind beneath the peregrine falcon's white eyelid
its wing is yours

Together we measure the acres of fallow land
we bear slowness into the foliage

Sealed by cunning our alliance is here

Pain is the other voice bringing us together
Accompanying me is this brambly hand

wandering over gardens with their gray stakes
breaking through the film on the well water

Astonishing as it passes by so familiarly

May some reed dust remain of words
an ash-spun cloth or these cuts
this edging of blood on your hand

You'll come you'll bear the yoke of foliage
your footstep won of pain

Jour du deuil

                    à René Char, le lendemain de sa mort

Le bras déboîté de la foudre
nul mieux que lui n'en devine l'approche

Nous l'aimons – son pas est l'unique mémoire
ses yeux lents vont remonter le jour

L'herbe croule l'herbe vivante

Day of mourning

> to René Char, on the day after his death

An arm dislocated from a thunderbolt
no one better than he can intimate its approach

We love him—his footstep is the only memory
his slow eyes will climb back up the daylight

The grass the living grass collapses

Seul avec le rapace à prononcer le silence
comme une plaie de feu sur les champs

En toi grandissent les épreuves de la parole
Mémoire ouverte – arrière-monde incendié

Sur l'enfant que tu épargnes
les couronnes d'air les couronnes de graminées

J'approche mes lèvres de ces lèvres
se dégrafe la rosée

Toute vie appartient au risque du sommeil
à l'enfouissement des songes

à l'éclat des terres sous le soc

Pèlerinage des pluies comme un égarement
pour nos yeux sur le point de guérir

Tu veux reconduire les bêtes infirmes
les voir passer le porche des sous-bois

et simples
défaire l'ombre d'un pas dans les flaques

Alone with the bird of prey to pronounce silence
like a flaming wound across the fields

The ordeals of words are growing in you
Open memory—hinterworld gutted by fire

On the child whom you spare
are crowns of air crowns of grasses

I near my lips to these lips
the dew unfastens itself

Every life belongs to the risk of sleep
to the burying away of daydreams

to lands bursting beneath the plowshare

Pilgrimage of the rains like a distraction
for our eyes about to heal

You want to lead the crippled livestock back
to watch them passing through the portal of the undergrowth

and as simple animals
undoing a footstep's shadow in the puddles

THE CALMED WOODS

Le temps s'invente un costume de brindilles
un faon débouche à l'orée

La bise tourne dans le dé de ses sabots
sa langue se souvient du lait
il saute les andins

Mémoire éclatée dans les ravines

Qui virent et virent sous la table du ciel
greffiers sévères – les martinets

Et nous – muets – déchiffrant leurs paroles
humiliés sans relâche
au souvenir des lèvres des morts

Nos yeux s'offrent à rassembler le jour
le jour cerné de flammes

Sucent les guêpes
la grêle de taches accordées par la mère

À l'Est elle veut cacher sa blouse d'épis
par où s'échapperait le cœur

Time invents a suit of twigs for itself
a fawn emerges at the edge of the woods

The North wind spins in the thimble of its hooves
its tongue recalling milk
it leaps over the raked-up hay

Memory fragmented in the ravines

What veers and veers under the table of the sky
severe clerks of the court—the swifts

And we—speechless—deciphering their words
are constantly humiliated
by the memory of the lips of the dead

Our eyes offer themselves up to gather the daylight
the daylight surrounded by flames

The wasps are sucking
the hail of stains bestowed by the mother

In the East she seeks to hide her wheat-ear blouse
through which the heart would escape

Écrire écrire seulement pour vous atteindre
Ô bois calmés

Il suffirait que je m'éloigne sous l'averse
avec au cœur les roses humides et la ciguë

que bouge à peine contre vos tempes
la cuve énorme du silence

To write to write merely to reach you
O calmed woods

It would suffice if I walked off in the downpour
with wet roses and hemlock in my heart

if the vast vat of silence
barely moved against your temples

Par les bruyères

L'attente

      Chaque soir, à la tombée du jour, tu marches vers le jardin ; tu viens là, près du mur de pierres sèches, reformer la couronne de cailloux blancs. D'un doigt peu sûr, tu redessines l'anneau d'air et d'amour où le tilleul se penche.
      Et chaque soir l'arbre abandonne ses poignées de feuilles. Le rouge-gorge, épiant tes gestes, te prête son œil de fronde.
      Résoudras-tu l'énigme du cœur avec ces mots de la terre familière ?

Toi la rive qu'effleure la lumière future
traînant ses manches de pollen

Moi le rêve du gravier d'eau

Orages acclamés par l'été
venez déchirer le fourreau des rivières
que brille un instant le dos de la truite arc-en-ciel

La douleur fraîche
tu sais la dénouer à mes poignets

Tu chantes — tes lèvres sous la serpe de l'eau
l'herbe qu'on froisse et sa pudeur

Il pleut pour que s'accomplissent les voyages

Through the Heather

Waiting

        Every evening, at nightfall, you walk towards the garden; you go there, near the dry-stone wall, to reshape the crown of white pebbles. With a hesitant finger, you redraw the ring of air and love where the linden tree bends down.

        And every evening the tree abandons its fistfuls of leaves. Watching your movements closely, the robin lends you his slingshot eyeball.

        Will you solve the heart's riddle with these words of the familiar earth?

You the shore just grazed by the future light
dragging along its pollen sleeves

Me the pebbly streambed's dream

Storms cheered on by summer
O come and tear up the sheath of streams
so the rainbow trout's spine will shimmer for a moment

You know how to unknot
the fresh pain at my wrists

You sing—your lips beneath the water's billhook
the crumpled grass and its sense of modesty

It's raining so that journeys may be completed

J'aime te retrouver à la lisière du jour
tu retires sa chemise au sommeil
fleur après fleur

Ni blanches ni mauves
les anémones tombent en silence
mêlées aux promesses et aux fêtes

Seule tu t'élèves dans la paroi de sang

La nuit nos lèvres étrangement complices
comme l'aiguille du silence oubliant de grandir

Unis pour savoir tout de l'épreuve mortelle
Ô cernes du bois ô touffes des myosotis

Les yeux dans les yeux – éclairés par le gel
et la fontaine et le parcours d'un seul oiseau

à une jeune fille

Embrasse sur mes lèvres – ô rêveuse
embrasse la longue patience du feuillage

Dans l'attente des pluies la chasse aux fouines
dans un vol de cendres brille encore ton secret

I love finding you at the edge of daybreak
when you're taking off sleep's shirt
flower after flower

Neither white nor mauve
the anemones are falling silently
blending with revels and promises

Only you arising in the wall of blood

At night our lips so strangely close and knowing
like a needle of silence forgetting to grow

United to know everything about the mortal ordeal
O rings on wood O tufts of forget-me-nots

Looking each other in the eye—eyes lit by the frost
and the fountain and the flight of a single bird

                           to a young woman

Kiss my lips—O dreamy girl
kiss the long patience of the foliage

While waiting for rain the hunt for martens
in a flight of ashes your secret is still shining

Ô toi le cœur fiévreux – arche sans lumière
descends toi vers le blé vers ses plaies
vers l'alouette qui les couronne

Guéris-les avec le vent et ses bannières
et toi plus dur par le chant deviens plus clair

Je t'ai placé dans la nageoire du monde
– oh la clarté que ce fut

Il y a trop de peine à te suivre maintenant
tu redeviens la peur malgré la neige
cette abondance de cristaux

Tu redeviens ce bruit d'os creux dans le rêve
ce fanion agité par une main de ténèbres

Ils viennent et se jettent sur ta bouche
ils flagellent et boivent cette eau-là
Suffocante
tu respires avec le fenouil du bord du pré
avec la centaurée grandie entre tes larmes

Ton sexe qui s'offre à la nuit
ton sexe n'effraie pas le chèvrefeuille

O you feverish heart—lightless arch
do come down to the wheat to its wounds
to the lark crowning them

Heal them with wind and its banners
and you hardened by song become clearer

I placed you in the world's fin
—oh what clarity it was

There's too much sorrow now to follow you
again you become fear despite the snow
this abundance of crystals

Again you become this din of hollow bones in the dream
this pennant waved by a hand of darkness

They come and throw themselves on your mouth
they whip and drink that water
Suffocating
you breathe with the fennel at the meadow's edge
with the centaury sprouted between your tears

Your vulva offers itself up to the night
your vulva doesn't frighten the honeysuckle

THROUGH THE HEATHER

Ils diront c'est peu d'accompagner les pluies
mais qui va nommer les fourches et le grès
qui s'occupera du frêne sans oubli

Les mots ne brisent pas leurs sceaux
Où je disparais tu regardes

Tes pupilles noires
hier accordées aux élans du fleuve
Qui les aveugle sous le capuchon des laniers

Si légère la terre n'est qu'une promesse

sa bouche remue dans la luzerne en fleur
les coquilles plus pâles que l'amour

L'herbe est venue se prendre à ton visage
Tes larmes ont la fraîcheur des prés

Nous sommes prêts – vers le seuil qui penche
vers les bois d'exil
– si peu de lumière nous suffit

Le soleil par taches effaçant nos bras

Aux semis ne parle pas de la douleur
ni à ce dieu des ombres et des sifflets de viorne

PAR LES BRUYÈRES

They'll say attending to the rains isn't much
but who's going to name the pitchforks and the sandstone
who without fail care for the ash tree

Words don't shatter their seals
Where I was vanishing you are looking

The black pupils of your eyes
in tune yesterday with the river's fits and flows
Who blinds them beneath falcons' hoods

The earth so light a mere promise

its mouth stirring shells paler than love
in the flowering alfalfa

Grass has come to take it out on your face
Your tears are fresh like meadows

We're ready—toward the threshold leaning
towards the woods of exile
—so little light we need

The sun effacing our arms in freckles

Don't speak of pain to sown seed
nor to this god of shadows and viburnum whistles

à Corinna Bille et Maurice Chappaz

Elles portent la neige à leurs épaules
et les mois et les années de neige
des moraines plein leurs bouches

À peine savons-nous les regarder de loin

Peu de signes – mais la bruyère en larmes
qui dispose le cœur à la nuit au partage
à d'humbles résurrections

to Corinna Bille and Maurice Chappaz

They carry snow atop their shoulders
and the months and years of snow
their mouths full of moraines

We barely know how to look at them from afar

Few signs—but the weeping heather
that lays down the heart to the night shared out
to humble resurrections

L'oubli

      Paroles que tu murmures à mon oreille, comme des ossements légers n'ayant plus même le poids d'une fleur.
      Tu dors, tu restes là, immobile, les cheveux défaits, un scarabée à ton poignet. Avec moi je demeure. Comment rejoindre l'aube, toucher à ces deux rives (la veille, le sommeil), atteindre seul la première Égypte ?

Visage au loin qui fut le visage
– et le même sang où battait le cœur

Ont disparu les travaux de l'amour
réduits à ces tracés crayeux sur la pierre
à des larmes qui brillent et ne brillent pas

Mémoire quand s'ouvrent les pages de la rosée

Les sauges – nous les avons laissé grandir
Qu'elles soient le signe et le pardon
qu'elles penchent dans tes yeux

sans que la marche s'interrompe

Oblivion

      Words you murmur in my ear, like bones so light they outweigh not even a flower.
      You're sleeping, staying there, motionless, your hair undone, a beetle at your wrist. I remain with myself. How can I reach the dawn, land on those two shores (wakefulness, sleep), arrive all alone in the first Egypt?

Face faraway that was the face
—and the same blood where the heart was beating

The labors of love have vanished
reduced to these chalky traces on stone
to tears shining and not shining

Memory when the pages of the dew open

Sage—we've let it grow
May it be sign and forgiveness
may it lean into your eyes

without the walk coming to a halt

À celui qui appelle tu ne sais que répondre
tu n'approches qu'un rêve d'orties blanches

Le feu couve – éclatent les silex

Sans honte nous restons face à face
unis par la pénombre et des arcs de ronces

Elles plongent leur regard en la maison
elles retissent ton manteau de cendres
et restent là demi-nues
sans peur
offrant la couleur de leur bouche

Oh comme luisent dans leurs doigts les ciseaux

Songe à délivrer la fauvette et son chant
creuse pour elle les chambres de l'air
ouvre une porte en plein feuillage

À genoux près des véroniques furent les mères

Songe à des mots clairs à des mots sombres
à ces mots cousus dans le tablier du silence

PAR LES BRUYÈRES

To one beckoning you barely know what to reply
you're nearing only a dream of white nettles

Smoldering fire—the flints shattering

Shameless we remain face to face
united by shade and the arches of bramble

They're gazing down into the house
weaving once again your coat of ashes
staying there half-naked
fearless
offering the color of their mouths

Oh how the scissors gleam in their fingers

Think of freeing the warbler and its song
of digging out rooms for it in the air
of opening a door amidst the foliage

The mothers were on their knees next to the veronicas

Think of light-colored words of dark-colored words
of those words sewn into the apron of silence

Ton corps nu ton corps abandonné
aux grappes des sureaux

Fièvres qui veillent je prends tes lèvres
Là-haut nous rejoignent les frêles éperviers

amour
brûlant à la nuit ses gerbes et ses gerbes

Tu t'endors dans la souffrance d'une femme
et tu veux lui sourire

Lentement son deuil reflue en tes veines

Elle dit les hirondelles criaient sous l'orage
nous avons mangé le pain près des ruches
à terre nous avons vu la moisson

La foudre à son œil perd son nom de folie
Toute parole se survit

1986-1987

Your naked body your body given over
to clusters of elderberries

Watchful fevers I take your lips
the frail sparrow hawks joining us up there

love
burning at night its sheaves and its sheaves

You fall asleep within a woman's suffering
and wish to smile at her

Slowly her mourning flows back into your veins

She says the swallows were squealing in the storm
we ate the bread near the beehives
we saw the harvest battered down

At her eye lightning loses its name of lunacy
Every word lives on

1986-1987

Of Screams and Silence

Des cris et du silence

To the inhabitants of Sarajevo—
so that they may survive.

Aux habitants de Sarajevo –
pour qu'ils survivent

Une écriture de pierre et de verre, le souffle prisonnier dans le cristal de roche, le mica, la sylvanite – à placer sous le signe de la mémoire, de la survie d'une humanité infiniment blessée.

Écriture née dans les ruines, y retournant, se déployant à partir d'elles seules. Psaumes brefs, sourdement éclairés par le sang, adroitement reliés, paroles à demi étranglées par le flot des larmes – tant de larmes !

On la voit suivre des yeux la cohorte des vaincus, des humiliés, des offensés. Elle songe le partage des peuples, déportés, assassinés à chaque tournant d'un siècle d'épouvante.

Écriture qui ne fera pas le deuil, elle, drapée dans l'infini du deuil pour cette raison que « tous les poètes sont des juifs », selon le mot de Marina Tsvétaïeva.

Et pas d'autres sens que celui d'une expiation. Elle longe le silence des victimes. Elle épouse chacune de leurs ombres. Elle demande pardon avec les dents et la glotte des bourreaux.

Écriture très secrète qui hante les lisières, les bois de bouleaux, établissant, rétablissant partout sur les vieilles terres d'Europe le cadastre du feu.

Écriture serrée dans la honte. Elle n'esquive pas. Elle devine les rêves de l'équarisseur. Écriture sur la neige avec le bois des luges, avec les pouces de l'enfant. Née fragile, aux commissures des bouches enfantes, découpures dans leurs voix d'hiver.

Écriture lente, méditative, elliptique. Hasardeuse, suspendue. Elle se plie aux pas du marcheur, elle s'accorde à sa respiration comme à la boue du chemin, aux battements du coeur comme aux fruits du verger. Elle accompagne les abeilles dans les halliers, les gouttes de pluie dans les haies.

Halte inouïe sous l'étoile qui vibre, nos yeux rayés de sel.

Writing made of stone and glass, breath imprisoned in rock crystal, mica, sylvanite—place it under the sign of memory, of the survival of an infinitely wounded humanity.

Writing born in the ruins, returning to them, unfolding out from them alone. Brief psalms, mutely lit by blood, ably linked together, words half-strangled by the flood of tears—so many tears!

We see writing watching the cohort of the vanquished, the humiliated, the offended. It ponders peoples being divided up, deported, murdered at every turn in a century of terror.

Writing that will not mourn, draped in infinite mourning because "all poets are Jews," as Marina Tsvetaeva puts it.

And no meanings other than that of expiation. Writing walks alongside the silence of the victims. It hugs the outline of each of their shadows. It begs forgiveness with the teeth and glottises of the executioners.

A very secretive writing that haunts confines, birch woods, drawing up, drawing up again the land registry of flames on all the old lands of Europe.

Writing tightened in shame. It does not dodge. It intuits the slaughterer's dreams. Writing on snow with wood from sleds, with a child's thumbs. Born fragile, at the corners of children's lips, bits and pieces of their winter voices.

Slow, meditative, elliptic writing. Risky, awaiting. It falls in stride with the walker, gets into harmony with his breathing and the mud on the path, with his heartbeats and the orchard fruit. It accompanies bees into the brushwood, raindrops into the hedges.

An extraordinary halt beneath the quivering star, our eyes streaked with salt.

Écriture humiliée chez les hommes : elle préserverait le silence, le non-savoir, les boitements du cœur, l'âme opaque et transparente – plus belle que les hautes herbes effleurées par le vent, mais proche des germinations, aveugle comme le sont les mottes en tous pays.

Écriture à remonter fleuves et rivières, en direction des sources tues, taries, crevant les ocelles d'huile, le bleu, même les cris des hérons – bonne tout juste à espérer contre toute espérance.

Écriture comme on partage le pain et le sel, furtivement, pressés de repartir, indifférents aux abois des chiens.

Une main, l'écriture, une main en voyage vers d'autres mains, vers ce lieu où deux ou trois sont réunis.

Écriture tressée de cris que l'on jette au visage du Maître de la vie et de la mort pour qu'Il hâte sa venue – et la délivrance.

1994

Writing humiliated by mankind: it supposedly preserves silence, not-knowing, irregular heartbeats, the opaque, transparent soul—more beautiful than high grasses lightly brushed by the wind, yet close to what germinates, also blind like dirt clods everywhere.

Writing to head up streams and rivers toward sources that have gone silent, run dry, piercing oily eyespots, the blue, even the squawking of herons—barely suitable for hoping against all expectation.

Writing as we share bread and salt, furtively, in a hurry to make off, oblivious to barking dogs.

Writing: a hand, a hand traveling to other hands, to that place where two or three people have gathered.

Writing woven with screams we throw into the face of the Master of life and death so that He will hasten His coming—and deliverance.

1994

In a Hay Meadow

———

Dans une prairie de fauche

To the silence watching over us

Au silence qui nous garde

y entre los seres que el deseo hace venir soy libre
y acaricio las tinieblas como una rama al agua

and among those beckoned by desire I am free
and caress the shadows as a branch would water

parmi les êtres que le désir appelle je suis libre
et caresse les ténèbres comme une branche l'eau

Homero Aridjis

Dans ma bouche les mots deviennent pénombre
et myosotis – syllabes de tendre lumière
pour celle que troublera le cœur

Viendras-tu saison brusquer les eaux froides
arracher leurs ailes aux petits faucons
ou séparer mes lèvres de leur sang

Sous l'écorce et la feuille mince du bouleau
silence tu t'abrites – et je m'abrite

Et toi pareille à la rose de l'ange de Silésie
belle tu es belle d'être sans pourquoi

Même les ombres aujourd'hui sont propices

Le blé va surgir et poser l'été sur ses tiges
pour toi qui doutes et marches haletante
vers ton commencement

Bûchers du silence – l'amour s'y découvre
instants éclats branches aux églantines
que brûle la terre d'été

Brûlent tes lèvres mes doigts qui les touchent
les saisons trop lentes où vont les rapaces
brille le nom tremblé le nom secret

fleur hier épiée entre les pas de l'eau

DANS UNE PRAIRIE DE FAUCHE

In my mouth words become penumbra
and forget-me-nots—syllables of tender light
for she whom the heart will disturb

Season will you come and hasten the cold waters
tear the wings off baby falcons
or separate my lips from their blood

Below the bark and the thin leaf of the birch
silence you take shelter—and I take shelter

And you are equal to the Silesian Angel's rose
beautiful you are beautiful in being without whys

Even the shadows today are favorable

The wheat will surge forth and place summer on stems
for you who doubt and walk panting
toward your beginning

Pyres of silence—love stands revealed
moments sparkles branches of wild rose
burned by the summer soil

Your burning lips my fingers touching them
the too slow seasons to which fly birds of prey
the tremulous name the secret name shines

flower spotted yesterday between the water's steps

Etoile lente à paraître – petite foudre
étoile guerrière lente à venir
foudre au nord du cœur

Traverse-moi traverse
la boue les neiges les moraines
les années d'aiguilles et de vent

Arrive seule dans l'offense et les pleurs
un sentier de faon aux talons

Mais traverse-moi viens frappe en secret
toi – la lumière froissée par la nuit
l'étoile saluée par le gel

L'herbe est un berceau et le vent ton refuge
Le soleil puis les ombres ouvrent tes doigts

Passent deux à deux les corneilles
tissant ton rêve et sa taie noire et blanche

Mais loin d'ici – et plus loin des souvenirs
flambent les renards – je suis leurs yeux

Une est la forêt – une bague pour toi

Slowly emerging star—little flash
of lightning warlike star so slow in coming
flash of lightning north of the heart

Radiate through me right through
the mud the snows the moraines
the years of needles and wind

Come alone into the offense and the weeping
a path of fawns at your heels

But radiate through me come strike in secret
you—the light rumpled by the night
the star greeted by the frost

Grass is a cradle and wind your refuge
Sunlight then shadows open your fingers

The crows are flying by in twos
weaving your dream and its black and white opaqueness

But far from here—and farther from memories
the foxes are in flames—I am their eyes

One is the forest—a ring for you

Tu es venue m'offrir un fouillis de branches
avec tes cheveux l'écorce noire et rose
l'odeur perlée de la résine

Soudain tu es l'œil et la durée des pervenches
tu te laisses traverser par la lumière
la sente le sous-bois

Le temps redresse et partage mes épaules
tu les noues à de lointaines pages d'herbe

Et ton corps délivré – barque aux aiguilles
plus lourdes et plus lentes

Tu es là rêveuse – immobile
à tresser la cage d'herbes du secret
Le vent hésite et menuise tes poignets

S'éloigne la bouche en feu de l'engoulevent

Ô fêtes de vent nocturne ô frêles papillons
des fougères montent et percent mes paumes

Le nom tour à tour rempli de verre et de suie
le sexe – la fraîcheur délivrant les sauges

mères immédiatement de l'ombre

You came to offer me a tangle of branches
with your hair the pink and black bark
the pearled smell of the resin

Suddenly you're the eye and how long periwinkles last
you let the light the trail the undergrowth
radiate through you

Time straightens and shares out my shoulders
you knot them to remote pages of grass

And your body has been freed—boat with heavier
and slower needles

Dreamy one there you are—motionless
while braiding the grassy cage of the secret
The hesitating wind woodworks your wrists

Moving off is the nightjar's mouth in flames

O festivities of night winds O frail butterflies
of ferns rise and pierce my palms

The name filled in turn with glass and soot
sex—the chilliness freeing the sage-bush

mothers immediately from the shadow

IN A HAY MEADOW

Tu vois venir l'orage toi prairie de fauche
et dans le galop des ombres tu seras toi
la bouche qui dit non et non

Elles fixent brèves leurs vols à nos yeux
les hirondelles à l'avant des pluies
délivrant la paille et la peur
au dos des mottes sèches

Elles crient pour suspendre nos larmes

Je t'aime – tu t'avances détachée de l'été
tu veux te joindre à la prière des morts

À chaque fois plus sombre paraît l'oubli
– les enfants nés linceuls et fumées

Ta robe d'amoureuse tu l'offres aux pluies
aux bouleaux – au soleil d'ici

Seule tu chantes pour la poussière

Pauvre je t'aime de venir sans même les abeilles

Visage à découvert sous la serpe de l'eau
visage aimé – avant les commencements

qui fut au calcaire aux écorces mêlé
et le plus proche le plus lointain

comme une offrande tue

You see the storm coming hay meadow
and in the galloping shadows you'll be you
the mouth that says no and no

The fleeting swallows ahead of the rains
briefly fasten their flights to our eyes
freeing the straw and the fear
on the backs of dry dirt clods

They're squealing to suspend our tears

I love you—you move forward unfastened from summer
and wishing to join the prayer for the dead

Ever darker appears the oblivion
—children born as shrouds and rising smoke

Amorous woman you offer your dress to the rains
to the birches—to the sun that shines here

Alone you sing for the dust

Being poor I love you for coming even without bees

Beneath the water's billhook an uncovered face
a beloved face—before the beginnings

which was blended with bark and limestone
and what is nearest and farthest away

like a hushed offering

Devant chacun de vous visages aux yeux salis
aux yeux rougis par le feu des larmes
je sais que les mots guérissent

Et ne pas approcher tes lèvres ni le violon
ni la blessure à ton cou

mais la courbe des épines musiciennes

Accepter que tu t'éloignes lumière amoureuse
que tu meurs aux vols d'oiseaux hâtifs
aux baisers sans nombre des pluies
à l'ouïe des montagnes

qu'un ange défait guide les pas et les pas
les paroles muettes soient l'unique certitude

Entre tes doigts médite la rose silencieuse
l'églantine allégée de tout secret

Au-dessus de toi harpes
tournées vers le désir les hêtres
où bruissent tant de paroles improncées

Reste muette quand l'azur fauche ses prairies
et les guêpes viendront boire dans mes yeux
la tendresse et l'oubli

DANS UNE PRAIRIE DE FAUCHE

In front of you each of your faces with dirtied eyes
with eyes reddened by the fire of tears
I know that words heal

And not to approach your lips or the violin
or the wound on your neck

but the curve of the musician-thorns

To accept that you—loving light—are moving off
dying to the flight of hasty birds
to the countless kisses of the rains
to what the mountains hear

that a defeated angel guides footsteps and footsteps
that mute words are the only certitude

Between your fingers meditates the silent rose
the wild rose lightened of every secret

Above you harps
turned toward the desire of beeches
rustling with so many unpronounced words

Stay silent when the azure mows its meadows
and the wasps will come to drink from my eyes
tenderness and oblivion

Toi que j'attends pour que s'achève la douleur
apparue de nuit avec le gel et les flocons
soufflée dans chaque cil de la forêt

fleur du fraisier sauvage – la plus proche
qui pesait la boue et les billes de chêne

et jusqu'à ce pépiement des roitelets
s'élevant de branche en branche
vers le faîte la voûte bleue
où s'apaisait le cœur

À l'heure où les montagnes se dressent
le feu de nuict à leurs chevilles
ouvert l'anneau des sources

Seul et seul
face au silence
ébloui par le ciel
loin de l'histoire du cœur
tourbe maintenant pont de laîches
tombe d'osier tressé par le souvenir

You whom I await so that will cease the pain
that appeared at night with the frost and snowflakes
and was blown into each eyelash of the forest

wild strawberry flower—the nearest one
that weighed the mud and the oaken logs

and all the way to the chirping of the wrens
rising from branch to branch
towards the summit the blue vault
where the heart was soothed

At that hour when mountains rise
the fire of night at their ankles
the ring of sources open

Alone and alone
facing silence
dazzled by the sky
far from the history of the heart
peat now a bridge of sedge
a wicker grave woven by memories

L'eau du silence – la belle eau
bientôt ne s'élèvera plus
tel ce mur
au fond des yeux
pour que tu l'aimes

Plus rien qui naisse sur tes lèvres
ni la parole ni la tresse des cris
aucun souffle
sauf les ombres étonnées
le fil décousu des violettes

Paroles qui volent pout toi lointaines
qui nagent à la proue des étoiles
voyageuses aimées par le feu

Paroles ce jour
qui reviennent effleurer mes lèvres
avec les herbes plus frêles sous le vent
les ombres lentes que peignent les roseaux

      Plus tard, c'est la rosée qui tombe ; elle touche secrètement nos fronts, nos lèvres – et nous approchons, libres de paroles, sans secours, la lumière aveuglante du deuil. Et rien jamais ne consolera le cœur, rien ne viendra le distraire.
      Les fêtes anciennes, demain, sécheront sur les grands prés. Les roches auront baissées leurs cils. Le vent caressera le vent.
      Tu prendras, toi, la forme et l'allure de la renarde quand elle s'éloigne au trot sur les sentiers ; je serai, moi, sur la rivière, la faux sagace des martinets.

DANS UNE PRAIRIE DE FAUCHE

The water of silence—the beautiful water
soon no longer will rise
like this wall
in the depths of eyes
so that you'll love it

Nothing more born on your lips
neither words nor the tress of screams
no breath
save the astonished shadows
the unstitched thread of the violets

Faraway words flying for you
swimming at the prow of the stars
fire-beloved travelers

Words this day
coming back to graze my lips
with the grasses frailer in the wind
the slow shadows combed by the reeds

    Later, it's the dew that falls, secretly touching our foreheads, our lips—and free from all words, helpless, we approach the blinding light of mourning. Nothing will ever console the heart, nothing come to amuse it.
    The ancient feasts, tomorrow, will dry on the great meadows. The rocks will have lowered their eyelashes. The wind will caress the wind.
    As for you, you'll take on the shape and speed of the fox as it trots away down the paths; as for me, I'll be on the river, the shrewd scythe of the swifts.

Et je l'ai su – alors tu me suivrais
toi la plus lointaine et proche
comme une étoile vagabonde
avec ses rires brodés
lumière à jamais
lumière parjure
serment de hauts feuillages
dans la transparence du cœur

Vite entrez dans la table des constellations
belettes feuillages et vous chevreuils

La boue fait voler ses sabots à mon visage
et mes yeux se murent lentement

Que s'en aillent les faucons
qu'ils jettent leurs cris aux citernes

Que s'accomplisse la douleur

And I knew it—you'd follow me
you the farthest and the nearest
like a roving star
with its embroidered laughs
ever a light
a betraying light
an oath of tall foliage
in the transparent heart

Weasels leaves and you roebucks
quick enter the constellation chart

The mud makes its hooves fly up to my face
And my eyes slowly wall themselves up

May the falcons fly away
May they toss their cries into the cisterns

May pain now be accomplished

IN A HAY MEADOW

Light and Other Footsteps

La lumière et d'autres pas

Aquì se està llamando a las criaturas
y de esta se hartan, aunque a escuras
porque es de noche

Here is where the creatures are called
to drink of this water even in darkness,
for it is night

Elle (la source) appelle là toutes les créatures,
et de cette eau s'abreuvent, quoique dans l'obscur
car c'est la nuit

Saint John of the Cross

Sous le vent de Tsarmine

Ainsi recommençait le voyage
non loin des fenils

dans le chant de notre chant
bleuissaient les lèvres du glacier

chaque mot
prononcé par ta bouche
arrachant aux pierres ses cristaux

À deux pas du gouffre – elles – fourbues
n'ayant plus à jouer les filles de l'air
les bras en croix sur les dalles
sitôt aimées des lichens

À franchir le col la lumière
follement dépeignée
sans cesse

mère sévère – elle saura les éduquer
avec cette part du vent qui glace
les coquilles et les bouches
visite le pain et le sel

Downwind from Tsarmine Pass

So the journey was beginning again
not far from the haylofts

in the song of our song
the glacier's lips were turning blue

every word
uttered by your mouth
tearing crystals from the rocks

A step away from the abyss—the girls—weary
no longer having to play at being girls of the air
their arms outstretched over the stone slabs
just as soon beloved by the lichens

Coming over the pass the light
wildly ruffled
relentless

severe mother—she'll know how to educate them
with that part of the wind that freezes
shells and mouths
visits salt and bread

Toi et le vent – vous montez la garde
jusqu'au seuil des constellations

Ici rougissent les nœuds de l'arolle
invisibles sont les mésanges
se feuillette le rocher

Nous parlons
le feu s'étonne et lèche le pain
des doigts peu sûrs retaillent les saisons

Aime les yeux qui ne cillent pas
– pitoyables façons de fourche

Aime celui qui murmure
bouche mêlée à la glaise du fleuve
en raison de nos faims et de nos soifs

Vibrent les anches des comètes musiciennes
pour qu'il parle encore avec les fous
juste au commencement
de leur peur

You and the wind—you're keeping watch
all the way to the threshold of the constellations

The knots of the Arolla pine redden here
the titmice are invisible
the cliff is flaked like leaves

We're speaking
the startled fire is licking the bread
unsure fingers are pruning back the seasons

Love unblinking eyes
—pitiful pitchfork ways

Love he who murmurs
his mouth mixed with river sludge
because of our hungers and thirsts

Make the reeds of the musician-comets vibrate
so he'll speak again with the insane
right at the beginning
of their fear

Abîmé dans le rêve – tu demeures
reconduit sans le savoir
vers les filles de mai
la forêt brûle jusqu'en ta maison

Dehors en patrouille les choucas
épointent rectrices
et rémiges

sans relâche
questionnent la face des vents

bientôt se nommera la pluie
langue hésitante et demi-phrases

bientôt les roches préférées
offriront leurs paumes
– miroirs obliques
à l'arc-en-ciel

Que je touche ces lèvres perdues
sur les seins les centaurées
un luisant de feuilles
à ces cuisses

Que je me couvre d'écailles
parlant avec l'humide

Attente – ô gestes froids
noués sous le soleil des aulnes

Que nage le cœur où nage la truite

Sunk into a dream—you're still
being led back unawares
toward the daughters of May
the forest is burning all the way into your house

Outdoors the patrolling jackdaws
blunt their rectrices
their remiges

relentlessly
question the face of the winds

soon the rain will utter its name
hesitant language and unfinished sentences

soon the favorite cliffs
will offer their palms
—oblique mirrors
to the rainbow

May I touch those lost lips
the centauries on the breasts
a sheen of leaves
at those thighs

May I cover myself with scales
conversing with moistness

Waiting—O chilly gestures
joined under the sun of alders

May the heart swim where the trout swims

Montagnes – chiffons humides
que serrent des poings et des poings

Les mots seuls inventent les pierriers

et la lumière à tête de faisane
vient poser ses plumes sur les sentiers

Un mot – un seul hors les langues
et toi qui touches son masque de givre

Chaque fois que tombe le jour
jeune fille tu t'éveilles

le torrent et ses bruits
soulèvent le linteau de ta maison

Tout sommeil est captif dans l'or des aiguilles

À hauteur de nos bouches s'est tenue l'épervière

s'est évadé l'essaim qui part à ta rencontre

Mountains—moist rags
gripped by fists and fists

Words alone invent the scree

and the pheasant-headed light
lays its feathers on the paths

One word—only one beyond languages
and you who touch its frosty mask

Every time day falls
young girl you awake

the torrent and its noises
lift the lintel of your house

Every sleep is captive in the gold of the pine needles

The hawkweed has stayed at the level of our mouths

the swarm has fled to meet you

Elle crisse la roue du ruisseau
pour cette veine qui bat à ta tempe

ce que fut ta douleur
nul ne s'en doute dans les épines

La tendresse serre l'été sur sa couche
fidèle au peigne lent des herbes
à l'eau aventurière

à toi

à chaque graine envolée de ta bouche

Si minces les Aiguilles rouges
à l'heure où naissent les papillons

au frère d'Assise
pour y coucher sa tête
tu laisses les pierres veloutées
tu abandonnes la saignée de ton bras

et tu demandes grâce et protection
accompagnant toute chute
sur l'aigle sur son dos
un vol de pierres
noires

LA LUMIÈRE ET D'AUTRES PAS

The waterwheel in the stream is creaking
for this vein beating on your temple

what your pain was
doubts no one in the thorns

Tenderness hugs summer on its bed
faithful to the slowly combing grasses
to the adventurous water

to you

to every seed flown from your mouth

The Aiguilles Rouges how thin they seem
when butterflies are born

so the brother of Assisi
may lay down his head
you leave the velvety stones
surrender the crook of your elbow

and ask for mercy and protection
accompanying every fall
on the eagle on its back
a flight of black
stones

LIGHT AND OTHER FOOTSTEPS

Deux purs enfants des bétonnières
poursuivant le décours de la nuit
tôt salués par le vent

leurs os – fracassés sur les pentes

Toi la neige salie
adresse au secret des montagnes
prières sur prières pleurs après pleurs

Toi le glacier presse enfin tes grappes
il est temps cette nuit – que le vin
coule et luise dans nos yeux

et vous les fleurs accourcies
qui fleurissez au seuil des névons
faufilez plus lentement l'ourlet du deuil

Ton nom – sueur à toutes pierres
non baptisées Seigneur des Grands vents

aux chemins muletiers
aux vires qu'étranglent les corbeaux
à l'air qui s'aiguise aux fleurs du glacier

une parole – bergère
rejoignant la nuit de tous
à l'étroit dans ses sabots de ténèbres

Two pure children of cement mixers
trailing the waning night
early on they're greeted by the wind

their bones—shattered on the slopes

You the soiled snow you offer up
prayer after prayer sob after sob
to the secret of the mountains

You the glacier at last press your grapes
tonight the time has come—may the wine
flow and gleam in our eyes

and you the shortened flowers
blooming on the threshold of snowdrifts
baste more slowly the hem of mourning

Your name—sweat to all
unbaptized stones Lord of the Great Winds

to the mule tracks
to the ledges strangled by crows
to the air sharpening itself on glacial flowers

one—shepherdess word
coming back to the night of everyone
cramped into its shadowy clogs

Hard down with a horror of heights
G. M. Hopkins

Sous le vent de Tsarmine – tes paroles
blanchies par les eaux du glacier
offertes à la moraine qui use
enfin immobiles

les touche au front la lumière sombre
sur elles se penchent les saxifrages
poussière et croix de sel

ici – tête contre l'effroi
bivouaquent les fils d'Orion

soudain le cœur veut s'arrêter de battre

Tu serres la clef d'une porte
où il neige et il vente

et tu veux entrer

en criant viennent les épaules
– elles seront caressées

ta bouche
va s'ouvrir sur le bleu
bien des jours avant le supplice

auront de quoi s'affairer tes mains

mais rester fidèle à si peu que la lumière
chaque fois qu'elle cloue et décloue
au ciel les vols de martinets

Hard down with a horror of heights
G. M. Hopkins

Downwind from Tsarmine Pass—your words
whitened by the glacial waters
offered to the moraine wearing them down
at last they're at rest

their foreheads touched by the dark light
over them bend the saxifrages
dust and a cross of salt

here—their heads against the dread
Orion's sons are bivouacking

suddenly the heart wants to stop beating

You're gripping the key to a door
where snow is swirling

and want to enter

while screaming the shoulders come
—they'll be caressed

your mouth
will open onto the blue
many days before the torture

your hands will have enough to keep them busy

but to remain faithful to something as slight as light
every time in the sky it nails and unnails
the flights of swifts

Ceux qui élisent le mépris
ceux qui t'ont enseveli
ignorants

avec les éteules avec les écorces
avec les douces chiennes
de l'ombre

qu'ils parlent – qu'ils se taisent

l'absence à ta hanche
tu t'effaces

à chaque pas
la bruyère s'avance en amie

plus tard est venue la neige
qui accueille la neige

Those who elect contempt
those who buried you
those ignorant ones

along with stubble with bits of bark
with those gentle dogs those bitches
in the shadows

let them speak—let them grow silent

absence at your hip
you efface yourself

with every footstep
the briar moves forward as a friend

later came the snow
that welcomes snow

L'unique défaut de neige

Les doux martyrs
ceux que blessent les myrtilles
que renouvellent les souffles de pierre

vieillards aux yeux de petit-gris
femmes aux seins top lourds
enfants de la mort subite
— les mutilés

Sans honte maintenant
qu'ils glissent et disparaissent
s'en aillent au-devant de toi Seigneur

Emporte-les cette fois sur une barque de neige

Je chante avec les pousses du froid
et les ramures et le noir d'écorce

avec la voix léguée par le père

Je chante et par le chant convie
aux abois des flammes
à la table de neige

l'autre et le semblable le frère
la sœur l'époux et l'épouse

Dans les champs exultent les corneilles
tirant sur l'attache des cris

cisailles en l'air haut suspendues

Mémoire — et cette grande faim du blanc
mémoire éblouie quand pleuvent
les aiguilles

Only Snow is Missing

The mild martyrs
those wounded by blueberries
those renewed by the breaths of stones

old men with snail-like eyes
women with weighty breasts
babies who die in their cribs
—the mutilated

May they now shamelessly
slip away and vanish
go in front of you Lord

Bear them away this time on a boat of snow

I sing with the thumbs of the cold
and the branches and the black of the bark

with the father's handed-down voice

I sing and through my song invite
with flames at bay
to the table of snow

those alike unalike and the brother
the sister the husband and the wife

In the fields the crows are exulting
yanking at their fastened caws

scissors hovering high in the air

Memory—and this craving for whiteness
dazzled memory whenever the pine needles
rain down

Nuit noire
la mère d'une étoile
secoue bracelets et grelots
ses deux mains aux pouces entaillés

et rester à son chevet et parler au silence
parler à chaque feuille qui se déplie
parler à découdre les écorces
aux gouttes aux lymphes

à l'âme pierreuse
dans son autrefois de lumière et d'ombre

elle – l'étrangère

elle muette – grès et fougères
cendres en fuite jusqu'à l'œil du potier

Laisse-moi tes yeux amour et leur silence
plus loin tes cris que je les cache
un à un sous la pelisse d'hiver

que je les pose dans l'espace blanc
les offre à l'inouïe dévoration
des branches

Oh la timidité de ta langue
– douceur de feuilles
à l'aine

le jeu des flocons mêlés à tes cheveux
sur la vitre le gel et ses nervures
si hautes les maigres étoiles
qui défilent

Black night
the mother of a star
shaking bells and bracelets
both her hands with slashed thumbs

and to remain at her bedside and speak to the silence
to speak to each unfolding leaf
to speak to unstitch the bark
to the drops to the lymph

to the stony soul
in its bygone days of light and shadow

she—the foreigner

she speechless—sandstone and ferns
ashes fleeing all the way to the potter's eye

Love leave me your eyes and their silence
farther off your cries may I hide them away
one by one under the pelisse of winter

may I place them in the white space
offer them to the incredible devouring
of the branches

Oh the timidity of your tongue
—softness of leaves
at the groin

the sporting snowflakes mixed with your hair
on the windowpane frost and its veins
so high are the sparse stars
parading by

Petite troupe à l'orée – les chevreuils
leur approche matinale – sauts
à réveiller le temps – gigue
à la cadence des sabots

et les bourgeons qui éclatent
sous les langues

Mais pour toi la fiancée juive
une seule coiffe de neige

et le vent qui la souffle

L'hiver veut baiser tes doigts
avec le lichen sécher tes épaules

toi tu retisses les draps
la terre au liseré noir les cendres
où les morts ont refermé leurs yeux

tu pries lentement de la prière des feuilles

This little troupe at the edge of the woods—roe deer
their morning approach—leaps
awakening time—gigue
to the rhythm of their hooves

and the buds bursting
on their tongues

But for you Jewish fiancée
a single hairdo of snow

and the wind blowing it away

The winter wants to kiss your fingers
to dry your shoulders with lichen

you're reweaving the sheets
the ground with its black trimming those ashes
where the dead have shut their eyes

slowly you're praying the prayer of leaves

Langue et nuit – une fois deux fois
trois fois soustraites au mensonge

langue et nuit – qu'elles soient fiancées
à la blancheur des bouleaux
aux parois du fleuve
au gel matinal

et qu'elles nous reviennent

Que les mains battent dans l'écorce
se réchauffent aux verdures
à la candeur du lierre

et qu'elles nous reviennent

Qu'il aille d'un trait
le cœur cerclé de fièvres
se prendre à l'aile du harfang

et qu'il nous revienne

Language and night—once twice
thrice shielded from the lie

language and night—may they get engaged
to the whiteness of birches
to the riverbanks
to the morning frost

and may they come back to us

May hands beat inside the bark
warm themselves in the foliage
in the ingenuous ivy

and may they come back to us

May the fever-ringed heart
spring up get snatched
in the harfang's wing

and then come back to us

Cœur – tu passes obscur
sous la pluie d'étoiles qui harponnent

Non moins obscur fut le rêve à gravir
cœur angoissé par sa nuit
cœur à sa fatigue

À la lueur du fer
va s'éclairer le paysage
se déploieront les fleurs du verger
un pommier agitera la fanion de ses gouttes

Rien
l'été se convulsant
à la commissure des glaces
sinon le souvenir offert à la gloire
sinon les étages sans fin de l'espace

Debout contre le ciel les granits noirs
et gris – stèles sur les charniers

plus haut dans l'air les fillettes et leurs voix
elles vont percer l'œil des papillons

Ô pitié – qu'elles s'invitent un jour à tes noces

Heart—dark you pass
under the shower of spearing stars

No less dark was the dream to climb
heart anguished by its night
heart given over to its weariness

In the gleam of iron
the landscape will brighten
the orchard flowers unfurl
an apple tree wave its pennant of raindrops

Nothing
the summer convulsed
at the commissures of the ice flows
except the remembrance offered to glory
except the endless levels of space

Standing against the sky the black
and grey granite—steles over the mass graves

higher in the air the little girls and their voices
will pierce the eyes of butterflies

O have mercy—may they invite themselves one day to your wedding

Dans l'œil il est toujours minuit
ils furent là – ils furent
ceux qui étaient là
rassemblés par la boue
leur peau nue pour vêtir le gel

Voici que l'on taillait
que l'on retaillait leurs os
et les barbes et le chant funèbre

Mort – fige à nouveau le sang
fige le sang où mûrissent les bouches

toi seule parle en l'honneur de la honte
ressuie la bave scelle à jamais le mensonge

Trop lents pardons – lointaine liesse
les jours étirent leur blancheur
dans l'immobilité du gel

Toi l'été tu t'es soumis au jeûne
tu renais à la mélodie des jeunes lunes

À l'abri sous le couvert tu écoutes
les avoines instruire la sagesse du faon
baigner les cils des grandes biches aux abois

In the eye it's ever midnight
they were there—they were those
who were there
gathered in the mud
their skin naked to clothe the frost

This is how their bones
were carved recarved
and the beards and the funeral song

Death—congeal once again the blood
congeal the blood wherever mouths ripen

you alone speak in honor of shame
wipe the dribble off again seal up the lie forever

Too slow forgiveness—remote jubilation
the days are stretching out their whiteness
in the frozen immobility

In summer you subjected yourself to fasting
you're born again to the melody of young moons

Sheltered and under cover you're listening
to the oats teaching the wisdom of the fawn
bathing the eyelashes of the big does at bay

Tueur – il a pris l'accent des branches
la brise dans les plis de sa robe
accompagnant ses vœux
le chant du loriot

Un baiser
– il recule suffoqué

la monnaie des constellations
rouille avec sa main

et la mémoire couche le vent du sud

Déjà l'aube s'est mise à ramper
autour des feux

où sèchent les habits de la trahison
où le cœur manque à l'appel
où nul ne condamne

Cris de neige dans le bois des luges
mienne la pente et miens les rires
tressés par les voix d'enfants

et purs jusqu'au profond du gel
purs leurs yeux humides
– le cœur
l'unique faim d'étoiles

là – tenir parole

Killer—he's taken the accent of the branches
the breeze in the folds of his robe
accompanying his vows
the oriole's song

A kiss
—he steps back choking

the coins of the constellations
are rusting with his hand

and memory is flattening down the south wind

Already dawn is crawling
around the fires

where the clothes of betrayal are drying
where the heart has failed to appear
where no one condemns

Screaming snow in the wooden sleds
the slope is mine and so is the laughter
woven by the children's voices

and pure to the depths of the frozenness
pure their moist eyes
—the heart
a craving only for stars

there—to keep one's word

Et pour vêtir tes épaules avant de repartir
non pas le foulard d'ombre et d'écorces
mais l'azur et les robes alezanes

ni les galops ni les hennissements
ni le vent aiguisant les fers
rien – rien ne va manquer
à la simple promesse

Comme ton visage s'emplit de craie
maintenant – qui fut le premier
inventeur des parfums
et des jours

ô myosotis dans l'orbe des secrets
quelle miniature fut plus douce aux prairies

Est-ce là ce corps de jade ou de jadis
et le même sang à circuler
sous la peau

est-ce ton visage plus clair
que le temps délivre sous les caresses
avec ces mains de plumes arrachées à l'aube

LA LUMIÈRE ET D'AUTRES PAS

And for covering your shoulders before you leave
not that scarf of shadow and bark
but the blue sky and sorrel hides

neither the galloping nor the neighing
nor the wind sharpening the horseshoes
nothing—nothing will be missing
from the simple promise

How your face now fills
with chalk—and it was the first
inventor of days
and fragrances

O forget-me-not in the orb of secrets
what miniature was gentler to the meadows

Is this the body of jade and days of old
and the same blood circulating
under the skin

is this your clearer face
that time frees by caressing
with these hands of feathers plucked from the dawn

De fleurs en fleurs
jusqu'au lait de l'alpage
nos rêves anciens remontent les pentes

tête qui traverse
à contretemps les éboulis

cœur qui bat
sous une enclume de poussières

Il peut soigner nos blessures
joueur dans l'axe des vents
le plantain

seuls les grillons dressent un belvédère
à la nuit – seuls ils restent à chanter
l'unique défaut de neige

From flowers to flowers
to the milk of the high pastures
our old dreams climb the slope

a head is rolling
off-tempo across the rockslide

a heart is beating
beneath an anvil of dust

Our wounds can be healed
by the plantain playing
in line with the winds

only crickets raise a belvedere
to the night—only they stay behind to sing
that only snow is missing

Dans la langue des fougères

Le ciel un dôme
les étoiles à la sauvette

sans défaut
les cris de l'enfant
où tu pénètres depuis toujours

sur la terrasse
le cheval à bascule
– son hennissement de bois

et toi l'oreille aux voix défuntes
seul et seul à genoux
humilié
serré dans les lés d'une aube étroite

Laisse amour
ton bâton piloter la foudre
vers les hautes forêts de mélèze

la douleur s'allégera
sous le fouet des fleurs

patience – les couleurs
seront confiées aux abeilles

À la fin les galaxies
auront lissé leurs plumes

envolées – ailes ouvertes
trouant le temps et ses frontières

viennent effleurer le contour de tes lèvres

In the Language of Ferns

The sky a dome
displaying stars

flawless
are the child's cries
into which you're forever entering

on the patio
the rocking horse
—its woody neighing

and your ear tuned to the departed voices
alone all alone on your knees
humiliated
cramped in the widths of a narrow dawn

Love let your stick
pilot the lightning
toward the high forests of larch

the pain will lighten
beneath the whipping flowers

patience—the colors
will be entrusted to bees

At the end the galaxies
will have preened their feathers

flown off—open wings
boring through time and its borders

come and lightly touch the contour of your lips

Pour toi compagne clandestine
une grêle de cailloux blancs
où relire ton nom secret

la parole
cherchant tes doigts
à l'autre bout de la forêt
l'anémone sylvie invente une clairière

mais quel silence amoncelé plus loin
veut glisser des pas de trèfles
sous le pas de ton amour
marcheur là-bas
sur l'asphalte des rues
oublieux des rites et de la promesse

À demi-mots – les mots de l'amour
terre et ciel et syllabes neigeuses
dénouées par ta bouche

et voir le cœur un instant
le cœur en son jardin de graines

voir soudain le pardon
courber la tête des graminées

voir que les bêtes ont soif
– dans le poème

Chaque soir plus libre
regarder le couple des milans
qui vient fermer le jour et ses peines

enfermer sa hâte
ses fièvres sous une double paupière

For you clandestine confidante
a hailstorm of white pebbles
where your secret name can be read again

words
seeking your fingers
at the other end of the forest
the wood anemone invents a clearing

but what silence heaped up further on
wishes to slip footsteps of clover
under those of your lover
walking down there
on the asphalt of the streets
and forgetful of the rites and the promise

Hints half-whispered—the words of love
earth and sky and snowy syllables
untangled by your mouth

and to see the heart an instant
the heart in its garden of seeds

to suddenly see forgiveness
bowing down the heads of the grasses

to see that animals are thirsty
—in the poem

Every evening to look
at that couple of ever freer kites
closing the day and its pains

closing up its haste
its fevers beneath a double eyelid

à Benjamin R.

Pour toi
l'enfançon
le tombé des nues
pour tes doigts de terre
pour que rêvent ongles et lunules

le collier d'osselets – blanc sur blanc
taillé dans la cascade

Plus bas ta mère debout
sous les paraboles du silence
elle inventerait pour toi la rivière

sa bouche aimée
vole et plonge et nage avec le cincle

to Benjamin R.

For you
little infant
fallen from the clouds
for your earthen fingers
so that fingernails and their half-moons may dream

this necklace of little bones—white on white
carved in the cascade

Further down your mother is standing
under the arching parables of silence
she'd invent the stream for you

her beloved mouth
flies and dives and swims with the white-throated dipper

à Maxime V.

Au secret
ivre de notre ivresse
sous les treilles du sang

le presque invisible
à nous précéder longuement
de ses grands yeux large ouverts

l'enfant né pour un baptême de lait
le sacre des regards et du feuillage

les doigts noués au gerbier nocturne
tant de fois surpris à se plier
déplier dans les eaux

sur quel arc tendu – le cri
de tous les cris le plus tendre

l'enfant nu l'enfant à découvert

visage aimé – avant les commencements
visage offert et dérobé aux grains de la lumière

to Maxime V.

In a hideaway
drunk with our drunkenness
under the vine arbors of blood

the nearly invisible
so far ahead of us
with its big wide-open eyes

the child born for his baptism of milk
the consecration of onlookers and foliage

the fingers joined at the nightly haystack
so often surprised to curl
uncurl in the waters

on what taut bow—the most tender cry
of all cries

the naked child the uncovered child

beloved face—before the beginnings
face offered to and hidden from the seeds of the light

Ô vous les bouches brisées par le pain
même dans l'exil parlez vos paroles
– terres lentes et soc de lumière

Partout sur les champs – tracteurs éteints
le jaune à foison les roues du soleil

Que les ombres cèdent toute fraîcheur
à la nuque des moissonneurs

Que sur eux tournent les ailes du vin
que le vent réinvente les faucons
retour de chasse

Bouches du rêve ouvertes au froment
– en souvenir – éparpillez le grain

Dans les campagnes s'embrase l'été
nous seuls sur le qui-vive
affamés de silence

Orphée guérisseur
au-dessus des lyres du sureau
et les génisses qui piétinent affolées

O you whose mouths are broken by bread
even in exile speak your words
—slow lands and plowshares of light

Everywhere over the fields—tractors stopped
the abundant yellow the wheels of the sun

May the shadows yield all their freshness
to the harvesters' napes

May the wings of wine veer toward them
may the wind reinvent the falcons
back from the hunt

Mouths of the dream that are open to wheat
—in memoriam—scatter the seed

In the countryside the summer blazes up
we alone on the alert
starving for silence

Orpheus the healer
above the lyres of the elder tree
and the panicked stamping heifers

La lumière – sa petite tête
à serrer dans ses linges de mica

dégage-la

Qu'elle passe silencieuse
au-dessus de la forêt et ses rêves de feu
surplombant la course des chiens et du cerf

Au fond de ses yeux – tu ne peux y lire

le sang s'égoutte
le crime est d'aujourd'hui
même les armes sont heureuses

la lumière – sa petite tête
à bercer dans la langue des fougères

The light—its little head
to swathe it in its mica swaddling clothes

remove it

May it pass silently
over the forest and its dreams of fire
dangling above the dogs chasing the deer

In the depths of its eyes—you can't make out meaning

the blood is dripping
the crime took place today
even the weapons are glad

the light—its little head
to cradle it in the language of ferns

Le fleuve en moi se couvre de roses
reste à épeler ce lent murmure
tresses lumineuses du sang
– rien que du sang

puis viennent les corps à peine devinés
– têtes et bras et jambes à la dérive

reste à chercher une sépulture
– pelles et pioches pour creuser le ciel

Une voix sourde passe d'une rive à l'autre
une voix de sable mêlée aux buissons
avec les œufs du héron cendré

s'élèvent uniques les pleurs de cette voix
très haut par les frondaisons

La nuit retombe en millions de gouttes

Roses are covering the river in me
but to spell out this slow murmuring
luminous braids of blood
—nothing but blood

then come the barely distinguishable bodies
—heads and arms and legs drifting along

but to seek a sepulture
—shovels and pickaxes for digging into the sky

A muted voice moves from one bank to another
a sandy voice blended with bushes
with gray-heron eggs

the singular sobs of this voice are rising high
through the vegetation

Night is falling in millions of raindrops

Des branches lâchent les buses
et le brouillard découvre les tombes

commencent les averses de prunes bleues

Au verger une jument promène les étoiles
son poulain galope à l'envers des saisons

Toi – je t'en supplie
ne dis mot défends la blessure
la bénédiction des lichens sur l'écorce

Est chez lui le cœur non vu non visité – tu

Être dans les pas des chevaux
et leurs crinières blanchies par le froid
et leurs pas plus lents sur les prés mouillés

ou le long des lisières immobiles
avec le loir ou le soleil chauve

à naître
à disparaître
dans la courbe des étoiles ocellées
Père de toute fin et des commencements

à l'abri d'une clairière là-bas
avec les colchiques et l'herbe rase
dans le tintement grêle des sonnailles
au plus lointain de la mémoire des feuilles

Branches release the buzzards
and the fog uncovers the graves

begin the downpours of blue plums

In the orchard a mare is taking stars for a ride
its foal galloping against the course of the seasons

You—I beseech you
don't say a word defend the wound
the benediction of the lichens on the bark

The unseen unvisited heart—grown silent—is at home

To follow the horses' hoof steps
and their manes whitened by the cold
and their slower gait over the wet meadows

or along the motionless edges of woods
with the dormouse or the bald sun

to be born
to vanish
in the curve of the eyelike stars
Father of every end and all beginnings

in the shelter of a clearing down there
with the autumn crocuses and the mowed grass
in the shrill jingling of the bells
in the remote reaches of the memory of leaves

Avec lenteur comme toi
les branches qui peignent le fleuve

dans le pays d'algues où marcher
à la lueur des étoiles – lune masquée

bleu de froid
un sourire au lèvre
le rêveur visant le plus haut souvenir
tirant à soi les yeux des bêtes aux aguets

soudain les cendres s'inquiètent du feu
brillent les désirs lointains

crépitent les buissons de la voix qui approche

Me précède ce jour la gravité des arbres
très grands arbres aux gestes lents
leur frémissement de feuilles
– cœur blanc

m'enveloppe la confiance du fleuve
l'énormité de ses herbages
ses huttes de brochets
le doux matelas du bois flotté

m'en allant vers plus d'absence
et d'autres seuils et d'autres lumières
ce petit lait des heures où tremblent les faons

DANS LA LANGUE DES FOUGÈRES

Slowly like you
these branches comb the river

in the land of seaweed where one can walk
to starlight—masked moon

blue with cold
a smile on the lips
the dreamer aiming for the highest remembrance
making his own the watchful eyes of animals

suddenly the ashes fret about the fire
remote desires glimmer

and the bushes of the approaching voice crackle

Ahead of me on this day the solemn trees
towering trees with slow gestures
their trembling leaves
—white heart

I'm enveloped in the trustful river
its grassy expanses
its branchy huts with pike
the soft mattress of driftwood

as I head for more absence
and other thresholds and other lights
this whey of hours where fawns shiver

Non plus ce cœur éduqué
par un seul arbre de cendres

mais le chant où tu patientes
lames aiguisées aux regards neufs
ton chant – et le silence qui s'allonge
derrière les pluies visitées par la rouille

1993-1996

Nor this heart educated
by only one tree of ashes

but the song in which you're patiently waiting
blades sharpened by renewed ways of looking
your song—and the silence extending
behind rains visited by rust

1993-1996

The Poem in Armenia: Notes

———

Le poème en Arménie: Notes

For Aroussiak

Pour Aroussiak

I felt like hurrying back to the place where people's skulls are equally beautiful in the grave and at work.

Je voyais qu'il me fallait au plus vite retourner là où le crâne humain garde même beauté au travail et dans le cercueil.

Osip Mandelstam

I

Pour traverser le dégoût – le mien, le tien –
son étendue – tes pierres, Arménie,
que je les compte et les recompte
jusqu'à la fin des jours !

et ce vert acide : le jeune blé
sur les collines de Dilidjan,

et ce mauve ou ce jaune :
tes alphabets de fleurs,

sur une route de montagne,
(mais tes routes sont tes blessures)
cette fumée : l'encens des poêles,
cette nourriture :
sept branches d'un chandelier de maïs !

II

Je veux baiser tes mains, Arménie,
tes mains d'avant l'amour et ses promesses.

Je veux tes pas humides vers tes autels.

Je veux m'agenouiller devant tes croix ailées.

Je veux que mes pupilles tournent en silence
– soleils dans tes roues d'éternité !

LE POÉME EN ARTMÉNIE: NOTES

I

To get through the disgust—mine, yours—
its expanse—your stones, Armenia,
may I count and recount them
until the end of time!

and this acidic green: young wheat
on the hills of Dilijan,

and this mauve and this yellow:
your alphabets of flowers,

on a mountain road
(but your roads are your wounds),
this smoke: the incense of little stoves,
this food:
seven branches of a candelabra of corn!

II

I want to kiss your hands, Armenia,
your hands from before love and its promises.

I want your wet footsteps heading towards your altars.

I want to kneel before your winged crosses.

I want the pupils of my eyes to turn silently
—suns in your wheels of eternity!

III

Enseigne-nous les neiges rêveuses de l'Ararat,
tes patois de vent et de pollen,
tes bergers d'abeilles,
– humble et souverain
l'art de promener les ruches sur le dos de l'Aragadz !

Apprends-nous la beauté – mendiante
de chaque jour – et des nuits,
elle veut baigner nos yeux,

avec ses braises brûler nos bouches.

Montre-nous tes façons de pauvre,
tes gestes furtifs, quoi !
jeter un semis de mouettes sur le Sevan !

IV

Et laisse-nous pleurer avec toi,
avec toi jeune fille,
perdue dans la « Vallée des larmes »

ou secouer tes jupes de terre
pour qu'il en tombe
les plumes
des huppes ou du tarier,
les notes aiguës de l'alouette
les herbes sages,
l'esparcette et le sainfoin,
la menthe, la camomille,
les nids de guêpes et de vipères,
– un peu de la poussière des morts.

et plus profonde à jamais
la mémoire des innombrables morts.

LE POÉME EN ARTMÉNIE: NOTES

III

Teach us the dreamy snows of Ararat,
your patois of pollen and wind,
your shepherds of bees
—humble and sovereign
the art of moving hives across the back of Mount Aragats!

Instill in us beauty—beggar woman
by day, every day—and nights,
she wants to bathe our eyes,

to burn our mouths with her embers.

Show us your poor woman's ways,
your furtive gestures, indeed!
sowing seagulls on Lake Sevan!

IV

And let us weep with you,
with you young girl
lost in the Vale of Tears

or shake out your skirts of dirt
so that from them will fall
feathers
of hoopoes or whinchats,
the shrill notes of the lark,
healing herbs,
esparcette and sainfoin,
mint, camomile,
nests of wasps and vipers
—a little dust of the dead

and ever deeper forever
the memory of the countless dead.

V

Arménie de larmes et de détresse,
je veux t'entendre rire de ton rire noir et bleu,
avec toi nous voguons, nous, rescapés de l'Arche !

VI

Arménie, tes cierges – et ce doux tremblement
de peau des flammes !

tu aimes et tu cajoles Marie - mère de Dieu
dans de très purs étuis de pierres,

même tes chants – tresses lourdes
s'allègent sur tes tombes !

Tu le sais, tu le devines : le Fils est l'Arbre de vie

mais tu n'en finis pas de couper le bois sec
de Grégoire de Narek !

Ô ses lamentations de siècle en siècle !
ses menteries confiantes.

Arménie,
juste avant que l'on te renie
vois, c'est ici que Jérémie a laissé son chapeau.

Et pour finir, vas-tu moquer les anges,
offrir des gages – être la réponse
du temps
aux bégaiements du ciel ?

V

Armenia of tears and distress,
I want to hear you laughing with your black laugh, your blue laugh,
we're sailing with you, we the survivors of the Ark!

VI

Armenia, your church candles—and this soft trembling
on the skin of the flames!

you love and cuddle Mary—Mother of God
in such pure stone sheaths,

even your songs—heavy braids
lighten on the graves!

You know, you sense it: The Son is the Tree of Life

but you haven't stopped cutting the dry wood
of Gregory of Narek!

O his lamentations from century to century!
his self-confident falsehoods.

Armenia,
just before you're repudiated,
look, here's where Jeremy left his hat.

And, finally, are you going to mock the angels,
offer proof—be Time's
response
to the sky's stammering?

VII

Arménie, tu te mires dans l'œil millénaire ;
sont tiennes encore ces découpes,
ces franges, ces lisières,

Arménie,
éternel atelier de taille sous le ciel nu.

Que ta langue,
consonnes de tuf et d'obsidienne,
voyelles de cerise et d'abricots,

que ta langue s'en aille seule au combat,

qu'elle seule convoque tes prophètes au cœur des villes,
et les saints sur les places, les martyrs dans les jardins,

ou rassemble des petites filles le long des routes
– cœur en alerte, cheveux au vent,
sandales et tabliers brodés,

regarde, une fois encore, regarde :

à peine effleurées leurs paumes,
les baisers-papillons nous raccompagnent,
Ulysse, nous, ses rêves, l'ombre des voyageurs.

Erevan, le 14 juillet 2009

VII

Armenia, you gaze at yourself in the age-old eye;
the fringes, the edges, what's left after the scissoring
still are yours,

Armenia, eternal workspace
for cutting up under the naked sky.

May your language,
consonants of tuff and obsidian,
vowels of cherries and apricots,

may your language go off alone to battle,

may it alone summon your prophets to the heart of towns,
your saints onto the squares, your martyrs into the gardens,

or gather little girls along the roads
—their hearts watchful, their hair blowing in the wind,
sandals and embroidered smocks,

look, one more time, look:

their palms only lightly grazed,
butterfly kisses leading us back,
Ulysses, us, his dreams, the shadows of travelers.

Yerevan, 14 July 2009

Y.

Y.

...in honor of this name of honey, light, and milk...

...en l'honneur de ce nom de miel, de lumière et de lait...

Io mi senti 'svegliar dentro lo core
un spirito amoroso che dormia :
e poi vidi venir da lungi Amore
allegro sì, che appena il conoscia

I felt awakening in my heart
a loving spirit who'd been sleeping:
then I saw Love coming from afar
so joyous I hardly knew him.

Je sentis s'éveiller au fond de mon coeur
un esprit d'amour qui dormait:
et puis j'ai vu de loin venir Amour,
joyeux au point que je le reconnaissais à peine.

Dante

I

Amoureux
de l'air – si près de toi
ivre de l'insolence des bourgeons

plus amoureux encore de tes poignets nus
que serre un nœud d'abeilles

là – sur cette route que bordent les larmes
seul – à l'abri des branches féminines

fier de confier le temps à l'œil des vergers
à d'autres fleurs secrètes et lointaines

loin très loin – là où se murmure le pardon
où s'élève l'encens des parfums juifs

II

Amour que j'appelle aux confins de l'Avril
dans les pierriers – par les sabots du cerf
jusqu'à la soif des lichens

tu traverses la douleur et son miroir

Que les pluies viennent te prendre par la taille
qu'elles célèbrent ton pas d'amoureuse
la menuiserie de ta gorge

et la beauté d'un regard aussi clair que le jour

I

In love
with the air—so close to you
drunk with the insolence of the buds

even more in love with your naked wrists
each tied with a knot of bees

there—on this road bordered by tears
alone—sheltered by womanly boughs

I'm proud to entrust time to the eyes of orchards
to other flowers secret and far away

very far away—where forgiveness is murmured
where Jewish perfumes rise in wisps of incense

II

Love to whom I call out at April's borders
amid heaps of rocks—with stag hooves
all the way up to thirsty lichens

you're going through sorrow and its mirror

May rains grasp you by the waist
celebrate your loving woman's stride
the carpentry of your neck

and the beauty of eyes clear as daylight

Y.

III

Et la seule réponse est réponse de fleurs
ou ce battement d'ailes d'un passereau
un instant – contre la vitre

mais vienne enfin la nuit
vienne l'heure de te mettre nue

quand se courbe le silence aux rougeurs de pivoine
que s'ouvre dans le lointain – le proche
le paysage de tes cris

IV

À celle que tu aimes à regarder
tu offres sur terre le trèfle des promesses
la vie sans peur – les quatre feuilles d'un songe

les unes pour le deuil – les autres pour la clarté

sans oublier le ciel – et ses passages d'oiseaux

III

And the only response comes from flowers
or these fluttering wings of a passerine
an instant—against the windowpane

but may night come at last
the hour to unclothe you

when silence bows to flushes of peony
when opens in the distance—what is close
the landscape of your joyful squealing

IV

To the woman you love looking at
you offer on earth the clover of promises
a fearless life—the four leaves of a dream

some for mourning—the others for clarity

not to forget the sky—and the birds soaring across it

V

Ô visage de luzerne et de mélancolie
ô faveurs des jours limpides

je te cherchais encore au milieu de la nuit
comme on s'agenouille dans l'herbe
la tête levée vers les étoiles

telle est ta grande douceur – le bois repris
par le bruissement des sources

dans les trouées du feuillage
la lune sèche – la lune printanière

VI

Tu venais seule à l'écoute des hautes fleurs
le cœur battant – seule à délivrer
le jour et la prairie

tu passais lentement vers l'autre rive

ô vierge sans voix – tête nue
libre - absente au front méditatif

et rien – ce murmure – le mot amour
oh comme il sut trembler sur tes lèvres

V

O face of medic and melancholy
o favors of limpid days

I was seeking you still in the middle of night
as one kneels in the grass
raising one's eyes toward the stars

such is your great gentleness—the wood taken again
by the murmuring of water trickling up

amid the gaps in the foliage
the dry moon—the spring moon

VI

You'd come alone to listen to tall flowers
your heart beating—alone to set free
the daylight and the prairie

slowly you'd cross over to the other shore

o voiceless virgin—bareheaded
free—a vacant air and a meditative brow

and nothing—this murmur—the word love
oh how it could tremble on your lips

Y.

VII

Tu tresses la corbeille des saisons – le miel
s'égoutte dans les branches

du lait de tes seins l'invisible blancheur
vient partager la nuit

plus tendre est l'écorce du rêve

et tant et tant de cris se perdent au loin

là – sous cette paupière nocturne – a voyagé
une enfance

VIII

Ou recommence l'enfance aux lèvres terreuses
jeune fille – je te salue – et j'embrasse
tes frêles doigts de fétuque

je saigne – et le sel vient sur ma langue

tel est ce voyage dans les plis de tes robes

sans le crâne des morts
ni la tristesse des lunes à tes genoux

VII

You're braiding the basket of the seasons—the honey
dripping in the branches

your breasts' milk its invisible whiteness
comes and shares the night

more tender is the bark of the dream

and so many cries fade away far away

there—beneath this nighttime eyelid—a childhood
has traveled

VIII

Or childhood with its earthy lips begins again
young girl—I greet you—and kiss
your frail fescue fingers

I'm bleeding—and the salt comes onto my tongue

such is this journey in the folds of your dresses

without the skulls of the dead
nor the sadness of moons at your knees

IX

Encore une fois les mains qui se touchent
paume contre paume
en souvenir des lèvres en feu

l'aube appareille vers les terres orphelines

et dans l'attente se ferment les saisons
les foins – les neiges
les pages ailées du blé dormant

X

Tendres syllabes de l'amour – en robe d'été
la honte vous assaille – la peur vous gouverne

personne qui vienne à votre secours

vous chuchotez dans la nuit

et celui qui s'éloigne entend ses pas le déserter

IX

Once again the hands that touch
palm to palm
in memory of lips on fire

the dawn casts off for orphaned lands

and while waiting the seasons come to a close
the hay—the snow
the winged pages of dormant wheat

X

Tender syllables of love—in your summer dress
you're assailed by shame—ruled by fear

no one comes to help

you're whispering into the night

and he who moves off hears his footsteps deserting him

XI

à la mémoire d'Antoine Watteau

Soit dit avec tes yeux de jeune fille – noirs
comme une rivière de fable – tu voudrais
humilier le silence

la conteuse pose un doigt sur sa bouche
et les mots étincellent dans la nuit

cerclent l'amande en feu

ta peau – la soie musicale qui passe
les eaux du jardin

au loin vont les cortèges

et celui qui écoute
derrière le mur du feuillage
se souvient des promesses de ton nom

XI

to the memory of Antoine Watteau

Be it said with your young girl's eyes—black
like a river of fable—you'd like
to humiliate silence

the storyteller places a finger on her mouth
and the words sparkle in the night

encircle the burning almond

your skin—melodious passing silk
the waters of the garden

in the distance the processions move on

and he who is listening
behind the wall of foliage
remembers the promises of your name

XII

De l'amour – ne parle pas dans la forêt
ni du pain moisi ni des pleurs

à force de t'appeler – beauté
là-bas – scintille un lac de montagne

le cerf y plonge ses blessures

il nage – il nage jusqu'à ton cœur

et toi tu vis
beauté – tu te courbes
seins nus sous les colliers de baies

et ton rire est un arbre

de l'herbe se noue à tes chevilles

les baisers – là-haut – se pendent à la futaie

XII

Of love—speak in the forest
neither of tears nor moldy bread

by dint of calling out to you—beauty
down there—a mountain lake is shimmering

the stag plunges its wounds in it

swims—swims all the way to your heart

and you're alive
beauty—you bow down
your breasts bare beneath your berry necklaces

and your laughter is a tree

the grass tying knots at your heels

the kisses—up there—dangling from the clustered trees

XIII

           à la mémoire de Frida Kahlo

Le cœur est cette montagne – où s'envolent
oiseaux et pierres

Ô toi plus tendre – plus belle que la clarté
qui fait trembler l'automne
aux vitres de ta chambre

L'enfant des solitudes est né pour toi

il veut boire le songe de tes yeux
il découvre des flammes
au secret
dans tes mains – amies des cerfs et de la colombe

XIII

to the memory of Frida Kahlo

The heart is this mountain—from which fly off
birds and rocks

O you more tender—more lovely than the clarity
that makes autumn tremble
on your bedroom windows

The child of solitudes has been born for you

he wants to drink the daydream in your eyes
he discovers flames
in a secret place
in your hands—friends of stags and the dove

XIV

Dans le cœur incendié – elle seule – la rose pourpre

en d'autres saisons je veux tes mains amies
plus secourables que l'herbe

même la pluie sous ses paupières d'aube

ton souffle à mon souffle mêlé

et rien que les fauvettes à la fenêtre le soir
elles vont et viennent – s'invitent
d'une berge à l'autre

et cette lumière des larmes
veux-tu – en cette nuit qui est la nôtre

XV

Pour être seule et nue devant moi
tu donnerais l'eau douce de tes mains

ton cœur comme une tombe de fleurs blanches

C'est ton rêve qui perce la pupille d'Orion
plus sévère – plus beau
que la guérison

XIV

In the fire-gutted heart—she alone—the purple rose

in other seasons I long for your friendly hands
more helpful than the grass

even the rain beneath its dawn eyelids

your breath with mine blended

and nothing but warblers at the evening window
they come and go—inviting each other
from one bank to another

and this tearful light
do you consent—in this night that is ours

XV

To stand alone and nude in front of me
you'd give the soft water of your hands

your heart like a grave of white flowers

It's your dream that pierces Orion's pupil
more severe—more beautiful
than being healed

XVI

Nausicaa – c'est toi – ô bien-aimée
qui t'enfuis dans le cercle des étoiles premières

Mars vient broder tes robes – poussières et cendres

Nous te verrons passer avec les lavandières
tu aimes et tu comptes les galets de leur bouche

tu réinventes le fleuve – et sans fin ses grèves
l'herbe de tes yeux – si bonne aux fous

plus tard le cœur – ou son effroi

et la patience au fond des chambres

XVI

Nausicaa—it's you—o my beloved
you're fleeing into the circle of primordial stars

Mars comes embroidering your dresses—specks of dust and ash

We'll watch you going by with the washerwomen
you're in love and counting the pebbles of their mouths

you're reinventing the river—and endlessly its banks
the grass of your eyes—so good for the insane

later the heart—or its fright

and patience in the depths of rooms

XVII

Sur l'autre frontière – de l'autre côté du fleuve
le vent discret parle des braises

le héron hésite – s'envole sur tes pas

et toi tu marches sans trêve

une voix murmure – où vont les jours
que deviennent les nuits

les herbes soldates
les grandes herbes répondent
nous sommes les Parques à tête de graines

Amour – nous veillons
nous retournons les brises
nous inventerons l'éclat – la nuit de ton sommeil

XVII

On the other border—across the river
the discreet wind is speaking of embers

the heron hesitates—flies off with your footsteps

and you keep walking on

a voice murmurs—where do the days go
that become nights

the soldier grasses
the great grasses respond
we are the Fates our heads full of seeds

Love—we're keeping watch
we're turning over the breezes
we'll invent the sparkle—the night of your sleep

XVIII

Toi – parmi les fleurs nées de la cendre
bleuets – bleuets par les blés tendres

Que mes mains redessinent ton visage
– avec ces fleurs nées de la cendre

mes lèvres – qu'elles retissent tes lèvres
avec le souffle d'une seule étoile

Que l'osier touche ton front – dans le secret
les eaux dorées du baptême

Ô bien-aimée
déjà la nuit se vêt de ta beauté
tu viens – sans hâte – tu traverses les larmes

tu regardes
tes pupilles plus légères que les fables

Que nul ne détourne mon regard

XVIII

You—among the flowers born of ash
cornflowers—cornflowers amid the tender wheat

May my hands refashion your face
—with these flowers born of ash

my lips—may they reweave your lips
with the breath of a single star

May the osier touch your forehead—secretly
the golden waters of baptism

O my beloved
already night is donning your beauty
you're coming—unhurried—across the tears

you're watching
the pupils of your eyes lighter than fables

May no one divert my eyes

Y.

XIX

Elle – suspendue aux larmes bleues
d'une hirondelle qui traverse la chambre

Le matin retisse le drap des caresses
essuie les boiseries de son rêve

ô douce mémoire que les taches sur sa peau
et quelle parole ajouterait à sa beauté

Mais le cœur – le cœur est le guerrier

XX

De son nom le plus tendre l'herbe déployée
et pareillement les saisons – minuscules
avec leur crâne d'oiseau

elle pleure si doucement
les vergers s'allument pour toucher ses plaies

et toujours les ombres – après son ombre
elles tremblent – elles se mirent dans l'eau du soir

XIX

She—hanging on the blue tears
of a swallow flying across the room

The morning is reweaving the sheet of caresses
wiping off the woodwork of her dream

o sweet memory her freckled skin
and what words would add to her beauty

But the heart—the heart is the warrior

XX

With its most tender name the grass unfurled
and likewise the seasons—minuscule
with their bird skulls

so softly is she weeping
the orchards flare up to touch her wounds

and ever the shadows—after her shadow
they tremble—mirrored in the water of the evening

XXI

Amour je sais – tu t'étonnes d'être cette femme
que la nuit claire et le vent – à leur tour
les étoiles – délivrent en rêve

en lourdes pages d'eau et de feu
dans la mémoire des puits

quand ton corps fragile mime la mort
– et l'efface

ton visage délie ses parfums

Tu seras toujours là – cette nuit – en pleurs
il n'y aura plus que le ciel – cette nuit
et contre le ciel – le dôme des feuilles qui penche

mars 2011-juillet 2012

XXI

Love I know—you're astonished to be this woman
whom the clear night and the wind—in turn
the stars—set free in a dream

in weighty pages of water and fire
in the memory of the wellsprings

when your fragile body mimics death
—and effaces it

your face frees its perfumes

You'll always be there—tonight—in tears
with nothing left but the sky—tonight
and against the sky—the leaning dome of the leaves

March 2011-July 2012

Voices in the Other Language

Des voix dans l'autre langue

Ciel sous les cris d'oiseaux

                                      Aus ihren Schatten
                                      herauf
                                      die ungesprochene Rede

                                      De ses ombres
                                      s'élève
                                      la parole imprononcée

                                                    Johannes Bobrowski

Dans mon chant l'herbe souveraine
l'herbe par les champs – l'herbe
aux crânes – l'oublieuse
des os longs

dans mon chant le dur travail du blé

L'âme aussi – de soins – de fatigue accablée
elle s'éduque – elle s'éveille à la patience
libre en sa mélancolie

aussi bien l'ancolie – heureuse
en sa défaite

le fer à cheval cerclant les saisons

et puis les larmes
aux heures lentes du souvenir
et tout ce qui s'échange d'une main aveugle

la cloche des morts – et son tintement de braises
là – pour finir – cascade sur le rouge des toits de tuiles

A Squawking Sky

> Aus Ihren Schatten
> herauf
> die ungespochene Rede
>
> From your shadows
> emerges
> the unpronounced speech
>
> Johannes Bobrowski

In my song the sovereign grass
the high grass across the fields—the grass
rising around the skulls—how neglectful
covering just the long bones

in my song the hard work of the wheat

The soul also—overwhelmed—with cares fatigue
it educates itself—it awakens to patience
free in its melancholy

the columbine too—happy
in its defeat

the horseshoe hooping the seasons

and then the tears
in the slow hours of remembering
and everything exchanged blindly by a hand

the death knell—and its embered tolling
there—ultimately—cascades over the red of the tile roofs

Si Tu venais
avec tes paroles – celles qui te précèdent

celles qui palpent le temps – devinent l'éternité

nos yeux s'ouvriraient – à ce jour de patience
nos pas réveilleraient les galets
l'un - puis l'autre

et le cœur – bondissant

quand s'écroule la falaise

sous les cris de cisaille
des cinq jeunes
faucons

Vivre de ce peu – de cette lumière de neige
de ce rien qu'offre la neige

avec cette part de certitude

un instant
au crépuscule
la tête redressée du chevreuil – ses cornes
fendent la lisière – tu suffoques

un souffle – rauque - abat le mur des buissons

If You came
with Your words—those that go before You

those that palpate Time—become eternity

our eyes would open—to this day of patience
our footsteps would awaken the pebbles
first one step—then another

and the heart—leaping

when the cliff caves in

beneath the shear-like screeching
of five young
falcons

To live off so little—this snowy light
this mere nothing the snow offers

with this share of certainty

a moment
at twilight
the roebuck's head raised—its antlers
cleaving the edge of the woods—you're suffocating

a hoarse—breath—blows down the wall of bushes

i. m. Seamus Heaney

J'interroge la langue des tortures
et seulement les souffles

au cœur de l'incendie
les grands arbres qui transpirent

et les bêtes – nous le voyons – elles s'éloignent
dans le puits silencieux de la forêt

et puis les morts – enveloppés d'écorce
ceux qui meurent dans la tourbe
ou collent à la sève

Je veux la langue de mémoire
nous l'écoutons – fiévreuse – elle se redresse

J'appelle sur les eaux courantes
la seconde en feu – où fuit le martin-pêcheur

in memoriam Seamus Heaney

I question the language of tortures
and only the gasps

at the heart of the fire
the tall trees dripping with sweat

and the animals—we see the scene—going off
into the silent well of the forest

and then the dead—enveloped in bark
those who die in the peat
or stick to the sap

I seek the language of memory
we listen to it—it is feverish—it straightens itself up

I call over the flowing waters
to the blazing instant—where the kingfisher darts off

Se perdre   se porter à la rencontre
de ces branches de frêne
l'hiver
de cette lune

toucher son masque d'effraie
lentement se vêtir des eaux gelées

Langage de poissons nocturnes
sous la glace – l'écriture
des écailles

L'herbe et l'hameçon aux lèvres
la bouche parle des mouches de l'été

du soleil – de l'ombre qui gagne les saules

de l'amour comme un feuillage dans le temps divisé

Getting lost—going out to meet
these ash branches
the winter
of this moon

touching its barn-owl mask
slowly donning frozen water for clothing

Language of night fish
under the ice—the writing
of fish scales

A blade of grass between the lips
a fish hook in other lips
the mouth speaks of summer flies

of sunlight—of the shadow reaching the willows

of love like foliage in a divided time

Sois digne de ta douleur – ne t'effondre pas
va – sur ce chemin – tête haute – mais
ne méprise pas ta maison
l'automne
étagements de feuillages et de vent

Bientôt la neige soufflera jusqu'à ton seuil
et celle qui vient du froid sera reçue

s'enflammeront les bûches une à une

Vous écouterez le silence – le cœur
intact – meurtri – continuera
de battre

Qu'aux boiseries se taillent les murmures
les caresses dans l'épais des poutres

et ce presque rien – des paroles – non su
le terrible *pourquoi* de l'amour
sera dit

Be worthy of your pain—don't break down
go off—on this path—your head held high—but
don't despise your house
autumn
the terraces of wind and foliage

Soon the snow will blow onto your threshold
and she who comes from the cold will be ushered in

one by one the logs will blaze

The two of you will listen to the silence—the heart
intact—battered—will continue
to beat

May murmurs be carved onto the wood paneling
caresses into the thick ceiling beams

and this mere nothing—words—unknown
the terrible *why* of love
will be said

Pour que je retrouve le lierre
les pierres qui cerclent ma maison

des deux côtés du chemin
respirent – en moi – les terres labourées

passent sur moi les lames – l'éclat des charrues

Quelqu'un – une voix – au devant des pluies
délègue les oiseaux

les halliers ne sèchent plus

L'enfance court derrière les chevaux
creuse la coquille blanche des millénaires

Demeure le souvenir de ceux qui sont enfuis
nœuds et cheveux – anneaux et bagues

leur voix – Tu l'écoutes traverser la discorde et le vent

So that I may find the ivy again
the stones encircling my house

on the two sides of the path
breathe—in me—the plowed fields

the blades come right over me—the plows are gleaming

Someone—a voice—goes out to meet the rains
delegates the birds

the thickets no longer grow dry

Childhood runs after the horses
digs into the white shell of millennia

Remains the memory of those who have run away
knotted hair and ribbons—rings and earrings

their voices—You hear them resounding through the discord and the wind

Tu habites le fer brisé
mais tes pas traversent l'eau de la rivière

À chaque fois les pleurs – tu reprends souffle
l'ombre d'un oiseau vole sur la muraille

Enfant – tu mettais le feu à l'herbe des talus
tu riais – enfant – l'eau et le sable s'aimaient - se devinaient

Tu ne parles à personne – la réponse – au secret
tu fréquentes le vent – nos fronts se touchent encore

nos mains invitent les fraises ou la girolle – le lait
du rêve a séché dans l'écuelle

Pas de mots – il n'y aura pas de mots

You live inside the shattered iron
but your footsteps cross the water of the stream

Weeping every time—you gather your breath
the shadow of a bird flies across the ramparts

When a child—you'd set fire to the grassy embankments
you—a child—laughing—the water and the sand loved each other—sensed
       each other

You speak to no one—the response—stashed away
you spend time with the wind—our foreheads still touch

our hands summon strawberries or chanterelles—the milk
of the dream has dried in the bowl

No words—there will be no words

Prends ces paupières – d'abord mes yeux
lumière des myosotis

dans mon bâton de marcheur – captive
la mémoire des sentiers et des routes

le blé de printemps – tu le sèmes

pour toi
l'avènement des gouttes
elles brillent – elles voyagent avec le vent

avant d'aller pourrir le bois chablis

Ayant retrouvé mes mains chanceuses
les galets filent à plat sur la rivière

l'enfant – à toutes jambes

là – sous la voûte de la hêtraie
il se mord les lèvres – il crie son nom

Take these eyelids—first my eyes
the light of forget-me-nots

in my hiker's stick—the captive
memory of trails and roads

the spring wheat—you sow it

for you
the coming of the raindrops
gleaming—voyaging with the wind

before dropping to rot the blown down branches

Having once again found my lucky hands
the pebbles skip flat across the stream

the child—running off

there—beneath the vault of beeches
he's biting his lips—he's crying out his name

La lumière – elle a ses fouets – cris de héron
qui tombent et tachent le jour

et nul n'y reconnaît son jour

Mais que tu viennes te cacher dans cette voix
parmi les arbres en fleurs – les roches nues
et les troncs – la langue des lichens
la houille au secret

Vers l'alpe – plus haut – aveugle
se détache la tête du coq de bruyère
une serpe de sang vole et tourne dans les sentes

mais que tu reviennes – toi – tes mains
et l'eau pour ma bouche

Toi plus humble – jadis à l'écoute de la parole

Light—it has its whips—heron squawks
falling and staining the day

and no one recognizes his day in it

But may you come to hide in this voice
among the flowering trees—the bare boulders
and the trunks—the tongue of the lichens
the coal in its hideaway

Towards the alpine pasture—higher up—blind
the shot-off capercaillie's head
a billhook of blood flying veering over the trails

but may you come back—you—your hands
and water for my mouth

You more humble—who used to listen to the word

En ce jour de mai le poème est du matin
il s'éveille dans les fleurs du marronnier

très tôt – dans l'autre saison
la neige le conduit dans la montagne

c'est là que le vent retaille nos lèvres
que le souffle nous revient

et là encore voir tes épaules sous le gel
les cristaux qui t'effleurent

oublier que je suis cet homme
que tu es cette femme

et voir s'agenouiller de nuit le Chasseur
Orion parmi d'autres étoiles

On this May morning the poem awakes early
among the flowers of the chestnut tree

very early—in the other season
the snow guides it into the mountains

where the wind trims our lips again
where our inspiration returns

and where I also see your shoulders beneath the frost
the crystals barely grazing you

forget that I am this man
that you are this woman

and watch at night Orion the Hunter
kneeling among the other stars

Les lilas – les noisetiers – les corbeilles d'argent
la pluie des graines ailées de l'érable
tapissant les sentiers

le lierre imparfait

et la peur – le cœur à vif
au secret des basses branches

Le sang de tes sœurs – blancheur de cygne

le soir – à la prière
les bras du père – griffés par les mûriers

Là s'élevaient les murs – et ta maison

The lilacs—the hazels—the silver baskets
the maple's winged seeds raining down
covering the paths

the imperfect ivy

and fear—the heart laid bare
in the secrecy of the lower branches

Your sisters' blood—the swan's whiteness

evening—at prayer
the father's arms—scratched by the blackberries

There is where the walls rose—and your house

Des voix dans l'autre langue

> come te, come te, signore
> noi siamo consegnati a quella morte
> che con più denti dell'amore morde
> e separa la rose
>
> comme toi, comme toi, seigneur
> nous sommes assignés à cette mort
> qui, avec plus de dents que l'amour, mord
> et défait la rose
>
> Cristina Campo

i. m. Christine Lavant

Étoiles – ô vous – les étoiles qui tissez le temps
jusque dans nos yeux nocturnes
étoiles à plis d'or – étoiles
sans merci

recevez la bénédiction
de qui sèche dans les peuples d'ortie

recevez le nom d'oubli
de qui se traîne aux genoux des chiens

la douleur entière
de qui meurt face contre terre

étoiles – ô délicates
faites simplement – ô soyeuses
que le bleu des sauges vête encore les vivants

Voices in the Other Language

> come te, come te, signore
> noi siamo consegnati a quella morte
> che con più denti dell'amore morde
> e separa la rosa
>
> like you, like you, Lord,
> we are summoned to this death
> which, with more teeth than love,
> bites apart the rose
>
> Cristina Campo

in memoriam Christine Lavant

Stars—O stars—you're weaving time
even inside our nightly eyes
stars with golden folds—merciless
stars

receive the benediction
of whoever withers among the nettles of humankind

receive the name of oblivion
of whoever grovels at the knees of dogs

the whole pain
of whoever dies with his face on the ground

stars—O delicate silky stars—
simply ensure that the blue of the sage bushes
still clothes the living

Sous la lune vague les branches de l'épine-vinette
elles tordent la saison de l'époux et de l'épouse
refermant leurs yeux mélancoliques

elles blanchissent le drap de la dernière nuit

branches nues et noires
le vent et la pluie vous secouent
vous demeurez les témoins de la terre heureuse

la trahison aura perdu son secret

nous écouterons les petits coqs de l'aube
ils s'appellent et se répondent

ils chantent l'eau – l'eau qui s'égoutte
et la lumière

Under the vague moon the barberry branches
wring the bride and bridegroom's season
closing their melancholy eyes

they whiten the last night's sheet

black bare branches
you're shaken by the rain and the wind
you remain witnesses of the joyful earth

betrayal will have lost its secret

we'll listen to the little cocks of dawn
calling out responding to each other

they're singing of water—the dripping water
and the light

i. m. Jean-Bertrand Pontalis

Près de la douleur d'un saule – toi – petite laine de pluie
offre-lui le silence – et que le jour s'en aille

Je ne sais plus qui s'est glissé parmi les tombes

Où est cette main – elle fermait les paupières
des morts qui redeviennent enfants

Les paroles s'entassent comme pierres

Je dis qu'un pâle haillon de lumière effacera la nuit

in memoriam Jean-Bertrand Pontalis

Near a willow's pain—you—woolen sweater of rain
offer him silence—and may the day depart

I no longer know who's slipped among the graves

Where is that hand—it would shut the eyelids
of the dead who become children again

Words pile up like rocks

I say a pale rag of light will wipe away the night

Elle descend vers nous la flamme des étoiles
mais la nuit s'enroule – froide coquille
autour du cœur

et plus trouble est le destin - un peuple se lève
pour le racket – la contrebande

Les bêtes affolées – les hommes sous le joug
dans l'oubli est la faim – renoncée la soif

Nos yeux déchiffrent la houille et l'ortie
ces rêves perdus – la terre marâtre

étirée – le long des berges

Les pluies – elles entrent par de hauts seuils
se déploient – oppressent le matin
se taisent

mais le cœur – qui l'arrête

Éveillée – tu te redresses
tes lèvres remuent – lents coquillages
bruits de rêves qui roulent sur la paume du temps

Deux corps unis inventent ce monde qui déjà s'éteint

Falling towards us the flames of the stars
but the night is coiling up—cold shell
around the heart

and murkier is destiny—a people gets out of bed
to extort—to smuggle

The terror-stricken animals—men under the yoke
hunger in oblivion—thirst relinquished

Our eyes puzzle out the coal and the nettle
those lost dreams—cruel mother earth

stretched—along the banks

The rains—they come over the high thresholds
unfurl themselves—oppress the morning
grow silent

but the heart—who stops it

Awakened—you sit up straight
your lips move—slow shells
sounds of dreams rolling over Time's open hand

Two bodies come together to invent this world already burning out

Si précieuse la poésie quand elle vient t'offrir
les ailes ferlées du faucon
son piqué de feu
sur la proie

Haute musique les arbres de lumière

verte la tige du trèfle – à ta bouche

Le vent est solitude – vaine sa compagnie
que défont les jours tristes

Sur un berceau d'osier se penche l'éternité

So precious is poetry when it comes to offer you
the furled wings of the falcon
its fiery dive
down to its prey

Lofty music the trees of light

green the clover stem—between your lips

The wind is solitude—futile its company
undone by the sad days

Over a wicker cradle bends eternity

i. m. G.-M. Hopkins

Naufragé de la courte Angleterre - ton ciel
se déploie – et – plus sûr que ses pluies
babil de paroles – nonsense

là – pure – s'illumine
la sphère de cris des exilées
parmi les mâts brisés – toute voile en loques

ou s'en va – revient – repose – unique
ta parole – se tient – droite
saigne – meurt

capitules des grandes marguerites

in memoriam Gerard Manley Hopkins

Shipwrecked on stingy England—your sky
unfurls—and—surer than its rains
babble of words—nonsense

there—pure—lights up
the exiled nuns' sphere of wailing
among the broken masts—every sail in tatters

where go away—come back—rest—your
unique words—keep themselves—upright
bleed—die

little tongues of big daisies

Éventails d'osselets pâles – le calcaire
à fleur de champs

ô mort – jamais tue – tes paroles

Énorme le silence – timide
le soleil n'est qu'une soie aux épaules

Défends – toi – la résurrection

Le cœur printanier s'arrête – suspendu

La hase en fuite – ces bonds sous le vent
ses griffes à peine – à recoudre les feuilles sèches

Hand fans slatted with pale little bones—limestone
surfacing in the fields

O death—never mute—your words

Vast silence—shy the sun
but a silken shawl slipped over shoulders

Defend—yourself—the resurrection

The spring-like heart stops—suspended

The hare flees—her leaps through the wind
her claws hardly even—sewing the dry leaves

i. m. Ossip Mandelstam

Barque à l'assaut des galets – ces bruits
sur la rive du cœur

Rose des foyers – bleu des fumeroles
les bouleaux pèlent sous le vent
piétinent les armées

La fauvette a pris feu sur tes lèvres

Dans son propre crâne – le temps
laisse tremper ses fanions

si peu profonde – la mémoire

et rien – nous n'aurons rien
pour éteindre ta soif de mourant

i. m. Nadejda Mandelstam

La parole et son goût de tuiles – buvant l'été
et le miel et l'amère certitude

Tu n'es qu'une visiteuse dans le souvenir
ailleurs l'aigre sueur des morts

Toi seule écoutes
égrener un à un les mots du chant

Ici le jour perce le tympan des morts

in memoriam Osip Mandelstam

Boat striking the pebbles—those scraping sounds
on the heart's shore

Rose of the hearths—smoky blue wisps
the birches are peeling in the wind
trampling the armies

The warbler is ablaze on your lips

In its own skull—Time
lets its pennants soak

memory—so shallow

and nothing—we'll have nothing
to quench your thirst as you lie dying

in memoriam Nadezhda Mandelstam

Words and their taste of tile—sipping the summer
and the honey and the bitter certitude

You're but a woman visiting memory
elsewhere the sour sweat of the dead

You alone are listening
shelling one by one the words of the song

Here daylight bores through the eardrums of the dead

i. m. Anna Akhmatova

Mais pour la solitude – tu embarques le ciel
tes larmes – de froids ciels de neige

Hier – les hirondelles
traversaient le vent des bannières
tu liais tes cheveux aux tiges des marguerites

Les jours et les nuits s'entassent dans leur prison
cinq par cinq se comptent les bâtonnets
que trace un doigt d'enfant

Dehors le temps – le joueur de flûte

Si pâle l'aube où nous verrons
de très haut – dans les rues – les ruelles
au pas plus lent des cortèges – derrière toi
un à un – vers la Néva – redescendre les morts

in memoriam Anna Akhmatova

Yet for solitude—you carry off the sky
your tears—cold snowy skies

Yesterday—the swallows
flying through the bannered wind
as you wove daisy stems through your hair

Days and nights tally up in their prison
the marks traced by a child's finger
are counted by fives

Outside—Time—the flute player

So pale will be the dawn when we see the dead
from high above—in the streets—in the alleyways
slowly moving along in a procession—behind you
one by one—coming back down—towards the Neva

i. m. Emily Dickinson

À la table des moineaux
s'invitent les miettes

aux rêves des fleurs
sont nouées les abeilles

Par grand froid – une main amie
tisse des habits de neige

un plaid pour l'enfant des cimetières

Rien comme ce mince secret – le tien
qui est – qui fut – le devoir d'aimer

car *la franchise est la seule ruse*

ou de préserver les cris
les pousses neuves du temps
le manque – dans la pierraille de l'éternité

DES VOIX DANS L'AUTRE LANGUE

in memoriam Emily Dickinson

To the sparrows' table
breadcrumbs invite themselves

to flowers' dreams
bees will be tied

When it's very cold—a friend's hand
weaves clothes of snow

a plaid blanket for the child of the cemeteries

Nothing like this slender secret—yours
which is—which was—the duty to love

for *candor is the only wile*

or to preserve the screams
the new sprouts of Time
the lack—among the scree of eternity

i. m. Elizabeth Bishop

Ténèbres intérieures – il suffit – d'une main de petite fille
je les cache – avec trois ou quatre épines du poisson
– un loup – dans ma poche de tablier

Espiègle est le jeu de l'esprit – un commerce amoureux

J'écoute les dés qui roulent et traversent la table
ils tombent à terre – je te les rends

bon – rien de grave – j'ai salué la cavalcade – toi
dis merci à ces grelots de bois

Les Fils du tonnerre se sont tus – tout ce que l'on peut
savoir – va – feuillette – l'Histoire a découpé les pages

mais apprends – là – épelle une fête de ballons multicolores
les rouges – les noirs – les gris – les bleu et blanc

chacun son étiquette – oh – je me disais - aussi
le destin – affaire de nœuds – et de ficelle

de Boston – ils partent

in memoriam Elisabeth Bishop

Inner shadows—suffices—a little girl's hand
and I hide them—with three or four fish bones
—a wolf—in my apron pocket

Mischievous is the mind's gaming—amorous dealing

I listen to the dice rolling across the table
they drop to the floor—I hand them back to you

fine—nothing serious—I've greeted the cavalcade—you
say thanks to those wooden bells

The Sons of thunder have grown silent—everything one can know—
goes—leafs through—History has cut out the pages

but learn—there—spell out a party of multicolored balloons
red ones—black ones—gray ones—blue and white ones

each with its label—oh—I was wondering—fate
as well—a matter of knots—and string

from Boston—off they go

Mis à part le sainfoin – les lilas – blancs et mauves
le chiendent – la caillasse autour de la maison

qui voudrait chanter le psaume
de bénédiction

réunir – ce jour – dans ses mains
les mains errantes de la terre en friche

La voix du passeur par-dessus les eaux les forêts

Une barque – soucieuse d'éternité
attend – muette – dans la passe du crépuscule

Tu sais bien l'autrefois de la chair émue

sexe et draps et sang se confondent

D'aujourd'hui sont les larmes
les yeux – les cils de l'ultime patience

Except for the sainfoin—the lilacs—white and mauve
couch grass—the loose stones around the house

who would like to sing the psalm
of benediction

reunite—today—in his hands
the wandering hands of the fallow land

The ferryman's voice above the waters the forests

A rowboat—concerned with eternity
waits—speechless—in the channel of twilight

You know well the bygone days of stirred flesh

sex and sheets and blood blend

The tears are today's
the eyes—the eyelashes of the final patience

Tu t'éloignes et je te suis – ô lune d'octobre
je vois briller ton épaule – ce feu bref
entre les branches

Gagne la nuit
la nuit que hantent les prophéties

Bientôt le cœur des villes est en flammes
le temps étouffe

si peu d'écume aux lèvres des suffoqués

incendiées – dans les hautes branches
les queues d'écureuil

Off you go and I follow you—O October moon
I see your shoulder shining—that brief fire
between the branches

The night is spreading
the night haunted by prophecies

Soon the hearts of cities are ablaze
Time smothers

so little foam on the lips of the suffocating

on fire—in the high branches
are squirrel tails

Pour France A.

Tu entasses les bouleaux de l'âme russe
le temps sans bord dévore les saisons

le vent – à l'assaut des datchas

Goutte à goutte l'or des clochers
tombe dans tes yeux
fidèles
comme furent la boue – les neiges

Tu salues la petite fille en lutte – elle seule
enfermée dans la cage des draps

en déroute dans le peuple des plis
elle doit se battre

imaginer le lourd – le furtif
au ciel mendier l'air et le souffle

oh retenir sur sa joue la main du père

ne serait-ce qu'un linge humide à sa bouche

For France A.

You pile up the birches of the Russian soul
borderless time is devouring the seasons

the wind—assailing the datchas

Drop by drop the gold of the bell towers
drips into your eyes
faithful
as were the snows—the mud

You greet the girl in her struggle
alone—enclosed in the cage of sheets

routed into a horde of folds
she must fight

imagine what weighs down—is furtive
begging for air and breath from the sky

Oh keep the father's hand on her cheek

be it merely a moist cloth at her mouth

VOICES IN THE OTHER LANGUAGE

Mais la beauté se ferme – au crépuscule
avec les fourches et le foin
les juments noires
– suspendu
leur tablier de goudron

Sœurs du soleil – suantes et pures
accablées de mouches
torturées de taons

Une voix vous appelle dans l'autre langue
une voix crie vers vous sur les champs
de peur que revienne l'oubli

But beauty closes itself in—at twilight
with the pitchforks and the hay
the black mares
—bags of fly repellent
hanging from their necks

Sisters of the sun—sweating and pure
plagued with flies
tortured by horseflies

A voice calls out to you in the other language
a voice shouts to you over the fields
in fear that oblivion will return

On rassemblait les étoiles – les bêtes de labour
l'air les rocs le sable les herbes fourragères
les sandales de fer et de luzerne
l'ombre des renards
le ciel mûr

Une main y mit le feu – le temps brûlait
au nord – au sud

Sur ces marches lointaines – effacées
à cette frontière
du rien

je cessai d'errer

Une terre – et nul ne l'appelle plus désolée
une fleur – nouvelle comme un point

détaché
le lys des champs
avec les yeux qui le déchiffre
reparut – posé sur un tendre miroir d'eau

We gathered the stars—the plow horses
the air the boulders the sand the fodder grasses
the sandals of iron and alfalfa
the shadows of foxes
the ripe sky

A hand set it on fire—Time was ablaze
to the north—to the south

On those distant borderlands—effaced
on this edge
of nothingness

I stopped wandering

A land—and no one calls it desolate anymore
a flower—new like a point

standing out
the lily of the fields
with the eyes that decipher it
reappeared—set on a tender mirror of water

Elles grelottent les perce-neige – caressées
prises un instant aux lacets du vent

si tardif le printemps
mais nos yeux sont lavés

nos pas sont des pas d'étrangers
à la traîne – derrière le dieu des Souffles

nos gestes – en lambeaux

Et que nos cœurs battent dans la cage d'os
toutes les nuits se confondent

Une image à peine – en croix – la vie
cette vie pour n'en faire qu'une
simple – ordinaire

une seule image à déplier dans nos yeux

The snowdrops are shivering—caressed
caught up for a moment in the wind's laces

such a belated spring
but our eyes are cleansed

our footsteps are like those of lagging
foreigners—behind the god of Breaths

our gestures—in shreds

And because our hearts beat in the bony cage
all the nights seem the same

Barely an image—on the cross—life
this life from which to make a single one
simple—ordinary

a single image to unfold in our eyes

i. m. Franz Kafka

Tu t'éveilleras dans la langue des vieilles villes
les friches – le vide – quartiers déserts
et noctuelles

avec les cloches tu t'éveilleras – tes ailes
de choucas cousus de fil noir

Et ton rêve a la bouche en sang – Kafka

quand le marteau de la cloche frappe doucement
tes tempes – assoupi – tu replonges

dans l'eau bitumée – les trop longues heures de la nuit

in memoriam Franz Kafka

You'll awake in the language of old cities
the fallow land—the emptiness—quarters deserted
and noctuid

with the cathedral bells you'll awake—your jackdaw wings
blatantly sewn with black thread

And your dream has a bloody mouth—Kafka

when the clapper of the bell beats softly
against your temples—dozing—you plunge

back into the asphalted water—the too long hours of the night

Nul ne traversera – ne percera le mur de l'aube
même pas le harle bièvre – ni les lames
du matin qui couchent l'herbe drue
ni le fugitif martinet
ensommeillé
perdu dans les plis du ciel

Eux – n'inventent pas ta route
ne touchent pas à l'abîme

Eux – ne cherchent pas de sépulture
nul besoin de pleurer – Cracovie

à la craie sur tes murs
récrits sans fin – les mots du ghetto

Reviennent – plaquées sur le dos du vent
masquées – plus secrètes
aux parois de l'air
sans fin récrites

avec les prières – *écoute Israël*
reviennent une à une
les paroles

de mort et d'exil

No one will go through—will pierce the wall of the dawn
not even the goosander—nor the blades
of morning that flatten the stiff grass
nor the sleepy fleeting
swift
lost in the folds of the sky

They—don't plan your route
don't meddle with the abyss

They—don't seek out a sepulture
no need to cry—Kraków

with chalk on your
endlessly rewritten walls—the words of the ghetto

They come back—clinging to the wind's back
masked—more secret
on the walls of the air
endlessly rewritten

with prayers—*hear, O Israel*
come back one by one
the words

of death and exile

Deux cadrans solaires – ni plus ni moins
aux murs du jardin jésuite

et si chacune des Heures tousse – hora
brevis – ultima
necat
le Temps s'estompe en minutes
au cœur tape et défile en secondes

Plus lent – sur son axe – le pendule
affole le destin

d'une pointe exquise
recadre les profonds univers

Alignées sont les roses au parterre – les braves
les sérieuses – toutes en lutte – se querellent
au seul regard de la Beauté

à la rose Réséda la rose Cléopâtre tourne le dos
la rose de Pangée – elle – se gausse d'Evergold

Au fond de ce jardin vont se perdre les pas

Se lèvent sur un tapis de fleurs défuntes
des pensées – suaves et mauves
pétales ailés

là – ne fasse jamais défaut que celle qui fut mienne
une seule et tendre rose – mais la rose Eperdue
elle – son grand châle de lumière gelée

Two sundials—no more no less
on the walls of the Jesuit garden

and if every Hour clears its throat—hora
brevis—ultima
necat
Time fades away in minutes
thumps in the heart and parades by in seconds

Slower—on its axis—the pendulum
panics fate

with an exquisite point
redefines the deep universes

The row of roses in the flowerbed—the nice gals
the serious girls—all of them battling—quarrelling
solely in the eyes of Beauty

the Cleopatra rose turning her back on the Reseda rose
the Mount Pangaion rose—she—mocking the Evergold rose

Footsteps will go astray at the back of this garden

Rising from a bed of withered flowers
are pensive pansies—suave mauve
winged petals

there—no one is ever missing but she who was mine
a single tender rose—but the rose called Forever Lost
she—her vast shawl of frozen light

Derniers plis de la promesse

> Above me, round me lie
> Fronting my forward eye
> With sweet and scarless sky
>
> Gerard Manley Hopkins

Quelquefois la lumière – l'hiver
et nous écoutons converser les neiges

elles bâillent les portes des ruchers
le vent s'y promène – tête nue

et rien pour les abeilles

ailes – alvéoles – dards – mandibules
– une seule et fine poussière

un peu de cire – trois fois rien
a coulé sur les hausses

deux sautes de vent
 et s'aggrave le silence d'Orphée

Last Folds of the Promise

> Above me, round me lie
> Fronting my forward eye
> With sweet and scarless sky
>
> Gerard Manley Hopkins

Sometimes the light—the winter
and we hear the snows conversing

the doors of the beehives are ajar
the wind strolling around inside—bareheaded

and nothing for the bees

wings—alveoli—stingers—mandibles
—just one fine dust

a little beeswax—next to nothing
has flowed onto the honeycomb

two gusts of wind
and Orpheus's silence grows

Même l'hiver se met à rêver

tes lèvres voyagent parmi les baies
le rouge s'empare lentement des combes

tes yeux se ferment
le cœur se coule dans les branches

et ces grands gestes de neige – oh si peu
regarde – l'adieu à des millions de morts

Nous restent les papillons du froid
et le petit bruit des sabots

des pas de hasard – les hardes sur la terre gelée

Tu vises plus haut que les saisons mortes
au souvenir des corbeilles de neige
où tombaient les rires enfant

Des branches mûries par le froid
tu retiens la longue patience

et tout ce qui vit encore

au pied de l'arbre ces pommes à terre
ces pommes gelées – tavelures

que vise l'œil des passereaux

DERNIERS PLIS DE LA PROMESSE

Even the winter starts to dream

your lips traveling among the berries
red slowly laying hold of the combes

your eyes close
your heart flows into the branches

and these broad gestures of snow—oh so few
look—the farewell to the millions of dead

We remain butterflies of the cold
and the slight sound of hooves

chance steps—deer herds on the frozen earth

You're aiming higher than the dead seasons
at the memory of baskets of snow
where children's laughter would fall

Of branches ripened by the cold
you retain the long patience

and all that is still alive

at the base of the tree these fallen apples
these frozen apples—bruises

aimed at by passerines

LAST FOLDS OF THE PROMISE

La beauté vieillie – la peureuse effraie
aux ailes déployées

que je la cloue avec son cri
sur le tronc de l'érable

que je l'offre au vent froid
à la morsure des plumes du gel

et partout ces loques – la nuit – ces découpes

Seules vont de seuil en seuil de timides étoiles
à peine guidées par des mains étrangères

Écris – là – maintenant
avec l'ongle cassé du temps
en la compagnie du froid – là – écris

avec la rouille sur le soc des charrues

le cheval
sa crinière en feu
l'étincelle bleue de ses fers

et les pluies

et les échelles de bois
(elles pourrissent sous les pommiers)

ou ce vol tendu des corneilles – d'arbre en arbre

Dessine encore – là – d'un trait sûr
à ta hanche – plus profonde
la blessure

Beauty grown old—the fearful barn owl
its wings unfurled

may I nail it with its shriek
to the maple trunk

may I offer it to the cold wind
to the bite of the frost's feathers

and everywhere these rags and tatters—night—these remnants of cloth

From threshold to threshold timid stars venture all alone
barely guided by foreign hands

Write—there—right now
with Time's broken fingernail
in the company of the cold—there—write

with the rust on the plowshare blades

the horse
its mane on fire
the blue spark of its horseshoes

and the rains

and the wooden ladders
(rotting under the apple trees)

or this tense flight of crows—from tree to tree

Keep drawing—there—with a sure stroke
on your hip—ever deeper
the wound

Se relève plus lourd le mufle de la nuit
l'eau des étoiles s'égoutte
– dans l'auge

Quelques pas – sur le pré
et nous respirons à pleine bouche
perdus – effacés sous le ciel sans limites

libres un instant – un instant défaits
là – nous rappellerons-nous
ce qui naît – ce qui meurt
à chaque seconde

des cris – tant de cris
restés – rentrés – noués dans la gorge

Heavily rises the muffle of night
the water of the stars dripping down
—into the trough

A few footsteps—onto the meadow
and with wide open mouths we can breathe
lost—effaced under the boundless sky

free for a moment—in a moment undone
there—will we recall
what is born—what dies
every second

wailing—so much wailing
withheld—knotted in the throat

Pour Grazia B. – R.

Après cette autre nuit
cet autre secret de solitude
tu retournes un à un tes gants de neige

vers ta maison tu marches – une rose contre la tempe

Et n'oublie pas ce que fut l'été du songe
entre le sable et l'eau – la grève et les roseaux

n'oublie pas le chant – les tendres syllabes
enveloppées dans leur coque

elles s'élèvent plus haut que nous

For Grazia B.-R.

After that other night
this other secret of solitude
one by one you turn over your gloves of snow

towards your house you're walking—a rose at your temple

And don't forget what the summer of the dream was
between sand and water—shore and reeds

don't forget the song—the tender syllables
enveloped in their shell

they rise higher than we do

Se penchent et grandissent les arbres du soir
les troncs – les branches faîtières
noircies par le froid

les seules à guetter l'ongle de l'oiseau
ou ces passages d'ailes grises
au bas du ciel

Ô trop humains – ô solitaires
ô candélabres muets

figés comme nous
au pied des jours de sombre lumière

à genoux – redressés dans l'attente sans mesure

The trees of evening bend and grow
the trunks—the branches roofing out
blackened by the cold

the only ones on the lookout for fingernails of birds
or those gray wings streaking across
the lowest section of the sky

O too human—O solitary
O speechless candelabra

frozen like us
at the foot of dim days

on our knees—straightened in unbounded waiting

Les boitements – l'épuisement du cœur
tout entier à sa fatigue

Mère – je t'ai vue l'hiver
dans cette neige poudreuse
que le vent d'hiver gifle aux vitres
je t'ai suivie par les persiennes de minuit

et tes mains – vues dans le jardin d'automne
elles taillent les tiges des fleurs fermées
la terre à nu – plus noire et plus légère
à chaque coup de pioche

Jamais mieux que dans le souffle printanier
plus libre – en compagnie de l'effraie
et ses vols brefs dans le verger

Sache que le cœur muet – ostensoir de la nuit
le cœur – oui – je l'ai haussé jusqu'à toi
ô tendre – ô mère sans gloire
du seul pardon

The limping—worn-down heart
wholly given over to fatigue

Mother—I saw you in winter
in that powdery snow the winter wind
slaps against the windowpanes
I watched you through the shutter slats of midnight

and your hands—spotted in the autumn garden
trim the stems of unopened blossoms
the soil laid bare—blacker and lighter
with each thrust of the mattock

Never better than in the freer
spring breeze—in the company of the barn owl
and its brief flights through the orchard

Know that the mute heart—monstrance of the night
the heart—indeed—I lifted it up to you
O tender one— O mother without glory
of the only forgiveness

Toi qui descends dans le désordre des jours
tiens-toi plus près de l'écorce
plus près du lichen

à lécher les calcaires

à marcher – seul avec la forêt

Noue telle colère à la crinière des juments
accepte maintenant cette boue sur ton visage

le mensonge – et sa roue de perles sur les tombes

You who go down into disorderly days
stay closer to the bark
closer to the lichen

and lick the limestone

and walk—alone with the forest

Knot that anger to the manes of the mares
accept now this mud on your face

the lie—and its pearly wreath on the graves

i. m. Umberto Saba

Encore si vivait un poète
un seul poète vivant
parmi les envols
du merle
l'herbe aux chats
les arbres centenaires

honteux
son cœur vide
simple jouet de bois
serré par des mains d'enfant

un poète qui sache
des paroles le périssement

ne tire de son chant que le grave

ne célèbre qu'une fille à sa fenêtre
et la corbeille de fleurs légères
où elle se penche

sauf – le sévère amour aux yeux de paon

la vie – à sa place

et la mer
immortelle – au fond de la rue
avec ses mains qui ouvrent ses portails bleus

in memoriam Umberto Saba

If a poet were still living
a single living poet
among the blackbirds
flying off
the catnip
the century-old trees

shameful
his heart empty
a simple wooden toy
clutched in a child's hands

a poet knowing
that words perish

draws from his song only the lowest notes

celebrates only a girl at her window
and the basket of simple flowers
over which she bends

safe—is the severe love with its peacock eyes

life—where it should be

and the immortal
sea—at the end of the street
with its hands opening its blue gates

LAST FOLDS OF THE PROMISE

Ce que furent étincelles et silex – blessures
et lendemains de fièvre

nôtre – le chemin des étoiles vagabondes
le vent – sa coiffe déchirée
le ciel – à bout de force

à terre déjà
le foin des solitudes – charrois
charrois qui penchent – basculent vers le couchant

Nous n'aurons guère su prier – à peine si nous fûmes
un instant – tournés vers ceux de l'autre rive
en pleurs – nos pas secrets s'en allant
vers d'autres tombes

Que brûle encore le temps – ou sa chevelure
ma vie sur les sentiers de montagne

tes gestes purs – et la roue des baisers

l'indépassable Amour
qui réunit la lumière et le vent

2009-2014

What were sparks and flint—wounds
and feverish next mornings

ours—the path of wandering stars
the wind—its breeze torn apart
the sky—no strength left

already battered to the ground
the hay of solitudes—cartloads
cartloads that lean—tip over towards the sunset

We'll hardly have known how to pray—barely if we existed
for a moment—turned towards those weeping
on the other shore—our secret footsteps going off
to other graves

May Time keep burning—or its hair
my life on the mountain trails

your pure gestures—and the round of kisses

the unsurpassable Love
that unites the light and the wind

2009-2014

NOTES

Unless otherwise attributed, all translations in this book are mine.

On Brief Death

(p. 15) **On Brief Death**. Homero Aridjis (b. 1940) is a Mexican poet and environmental activist. The epigraph quotes lines from his poem "Quemar las naves" ("Burning One's Ships" and sometimes translated metaphorically as "Burning One's Bridges"). See his collection *Quemar las naves* (Ed. Joaquín Mortiz, México, 1975).

(p. 17) "I. Whiter than Salt." The "Comedy of Thirst" mentioned in the second sentence alludes to Arthur Rimbaud's poem "Comédie de la soif" (1872), which begins "We are your Grandparents, the Grownups! / Covered with cold sweat / Of the moon and the vegetation". In this poem, Rimbaud dialogues with his grandparents who have "come back from the cemetery" and tell him to "take the liquors from our cupboards; / Tea and Coffee, so rare, are singing in the kettles." "Ah! to drink all the urns dry!" he concludes.

(p. 37) **The Bony Night**. Pierre-Jean Jouve (1887-1976), the French poet and novelist. The first full edition of the poetry collection *La Vierge de Paris* was published in 1946.

The Calmed Woods

(p. 51) The epigraph by the French poet Pierre-Albert Jourdan (1924-1981) is drawn from his book *Fragments* (Paris: Éditions de L'Ermitage, 1979), which was republished in *Les Sandales de paille* (Paris: Mercure de France, 1987). The aphorism is not included in my translation, *The Straw Sandals: Selected Prose and Poetry* (New York: Chelsea Editions, 2011).

(p. 69) **Night of November First**. This section is dedicated to Paul Celan (1920-1970), the German-language poet. The epigraph "nunc dimittis" literally means "now you dismiss" and refers to the Song of Simeon (sometimes called the Canticle of Simeon), Luke 2:29-32. The sense of the first line of the song, in Latin, "Nunc dimittis servum tuum, Domine, secundum verbum tuum in pace," means "Now, Lord, let Thy servant, according to Thy word, depart in peace." Celan committed suicide by jumping into the Seine. This is alluded to in the last line of the first poem of this section. November First is All Saints' Day for Catholics.

(p. 69) "For us your bread is upside down." Bread turned upside down is considered unlucky, an evil omen.

(p. 75) "and blended with canal locks wheels of watermills." Voélin is thinking of the Plain of Alsace or of Burgundy with the Rhone-Rhine Canal, the places where he first saw locks as a child.

(p. 75) "Look—the grieving driftwood is coming apart." Voélin has given me this explanation of the French original, "Vois – le bois du deuil se disloque": "Maybe driftwood, deadwood heaped up, a mass that comes undone because of the current, the force of flowing water, the force of movement, that is, life that doesn't tolerate mourning very long."

(p. 81) **The Calmed Woods.** Pierre Chappuis, the Swiss poet (b. 1930), is a close friend of Pierre Voélin's. A vast selection of his writing is available in my translation, *Like Bits of Wind: Selected Poetry and Poetic Prose 1974-2014* (Seagull Books, 2016).

(p. 83) "Day of Mourning" is dedicated to the French poet René Char (1907-1988). Since Char died on February 19, 1988, this poem was written on February 20, 2016.

(p. 99) Corinna Bille (1912-1979) and Maurice Chappaz (1916-2009), who were married, are two important Swiss writers.

(p. 105) At the end of the sequence, Voélin adds this note: "Les Bois Calmés (literally, 'The Calmed Woods') is a locality that can be found on a map of France, somewhere in Franche-Comté."

Of Screams and Silence

(p. 107) This text, written in 1994, was later published in *La Nuit accoutumée* (2002). The epigraph refers to the Yugoslav Wars, when Sarajevo, the capital of Bosnia, was besieged by the Serbian Army. The Russian poet Marina Tsvetaeva (1892-1941) is mentioned in the text. She long lived in exile from the Soviet Union; when she returned in 1939, she survived for a while in utter poverty, having been refused all aid from Stalin's government; she eventually hanged herself. Paul Celan admired Tsvetaeva's poetry, although he never translated it. He uses her line "All poets are Jews" as the epigraph to his poem "Und mit dem Buch aus Tarussa" (*Niemandsrose*, 1963). Tsvetaeva's line can be found in her "Poem of the End" (1924), where it actually reads "[In this most Christian world], the poets are Yids!" There is a fascinating discussion of Celan's epigraph in Christine Ivanovic's article "All Poets are Jews": Paul Celan's "Readings of Marina Tsvetayeva" (*Glossen : Literatur und Kultur in den deutschsprachigen Ländern nach 1945*, volume 6, 1999).

(p. 109) "A very secretive writing that haunts confines, birch woods, drawing up, drawing up ever again the land registry of flames over all the old lands of Europe." The "birch woods" here recall the concentration camp Auschwitz-Birkenau, for the place name "Birkenau" is based on the German word "Birke" (birch). The image also relates to the tree often associated with Russia and thus the Soviet Union. With the word "confines" (in French, "lisières," which also means the "edges" of woods), Voélin is referring to borders and thus escaping.

(p. 111) "oily eyespots," in French "les ocelles d'huile." The French term "ocelle" refers to peacock eyespots, and the poet associates them here, as he has explained to me, with those multicolored spots of oil that grow into circles, when the rain falls, and come to resemble colored concentric targets.

In a Hay Meadow

(p. 113) This sequence forms the middle section of *Parole et famine* (1995) and was slightly revised by the poet in February 2015. This translation takes into account the poet's revisions. The epigraph by the aforementioned Mexican poet Homero Aridjis is drawn from his *Los Espacios azules* (Ed. Joaquín Mortiz, 1969), a book available in English as *Blue Spaces: Selected Poems* (Seabury Press, 1974).

(p. 115) "And you are equal to the Silesian Angel's rose / beautiful you are beautiful in being without whys" is a reference to the German mystical poet Angelus Silesius (1624-1677), a Lutheran who converted to Catholicism in 1654. Voélin alludes to a comment made by Jorge Luis Borges (1899-1986) in one of his lectures from *Siete Noches* (1980), as translated by Eliot Weinberger in *Seven Nights* (New Directions, 1994): "I will end with a great line by the poet who, in the seventeenth century, took the strangely real and poetic name of Angelus Silesius. It is the summary of all I have said tonight — except that I have said it by means of reasoning and simulated reasoning. I will say it first in Spanish and then in German: 'La rosa es sin porqué; florece porque florece. Die Rose ist ohne warum; sie blühet weil sie blühet.'" The line, which comes from Angelus Silesius's *The Cherubinic Pilgrim* (1657), means "The Rose is without a why; it blooms because it blooms."

(p. 124) "le feu de nuict". The phrase is taken from the poem "CCCLV" in *Délie* by Maurice Scève (ca. 1500-ca. 1560). Here are the first four lines of the poem: "L'Aulbe venant pour nous rendre apparent / Ce, que l'obscur des ténèbres nous cèle, / Le feu de nuict en mon corps transparent, / Rentre en mon cœur, couvrant mainte estincelle" ("The Dawn coming to make apparent to us / What the darkness of the shadows hides, / The fire of the night in my transparent body, / Comes back to my heart, covering many a spark"). In the 1980s, Pierre Voélin briefly ran a small press, called Le Feu de Nuict, with the Swiss poet Frédéric Wandelère.

Light and other Footsteps

(p. 131) Since the publication of this book in 1997, Voélin has slightly modified the original French texts in a few places. These changes have been taken into account here. The epigraph "Aquì se està llamando a las criaturas. . ." is from Saint John of the Cross's "Cantar del alma que se que se huelga de conocer a Dios por fe" ["Song of the Soul that Rejoices in Knowing God through Faith"].

(p. 133) Tsarmine is a locality in the Valais part of Switzerland. It is a rather steep pass between two Alpine regions, the Val d'Arolla and the Vallon de Ferpècle.

(p. 141) The Aiguilles Rouges is a mountainous massif near Chamonix and on the other side of the valley from the Mont Blanc.

(p. 143) "blooming on the threshold of snowdrifts." In French, the word "névon" recalls René Char (1907-1988) because of the family mansion, called "Les Névons," in which he was born and grew up, and because of his long poem "La Deuil des Névons" in his book *La Parole en archipel* (1962).

(p. 145) The epigraph "Hard down with a horror of heights" by Gerard Manley Hopkins (1844-1889) is from "The Wreck of the Deutschland," *The Poems of Gerard Manley Hopkins*, Oxford / New York: Oxford University Press, 4th edition, 1967, strophe 2, p. 52.

(p. 149) "go in front of you Lord." Of the aforementioned changes made by the poet to the printed version of this book, this line represents the one important modification, since the initial version was "s'en aillent au-devant de toi chaleur": thus "warmth" and not "Lord."

The Poem in Armenia: Notes

(p. 187) This poem, written in 2009 after the poet's trip to Armenia, was published in the review *L'Étrangère* (Spring 2016), along with the following explanation, dated March 27, 2010:

> "Last summer I went to Armenia; in 1973, I had read André du Bouchet's translation published under the penname of Louis Bruzon—we were in the midst of the cold war—of Osip Mandelstam's beautiful *Voyage en Arménie* [Journey to Armenia].
> And, of course, the desire quickly took shape in my mind to visit one day this country that is at once near and faraway—I was twenty-four years old; a country about which I thus intensely dreamt, yet in the manner of the Apostle Thomas: I had to touch it in order to believe—the wounds, that is, touch the flowers, the stones, and then see, with my own eyes, those bird-like peoples weaving the nest of a country as incredible as a Biblical vision.
> This is how the poem written here was born, on the shore of Lake Sevan.
> I must also excuse myself for the kind of fervor permeating this poem, an almost shameful fervor since such feelings are so rarely expressed in contemporary poetry; but I think that this fervor is mine as much as it was Mandelstam's in the Spring of 1930, indeed for reasons other than those that stirred me; and I have no trouble believing that this fervor was also felt by his remarkable translator."

The epigraph is borrowed from Mandelstam's *Voyage to Armenia,* "III. Zamoskvorechie," translated by Clarence Brown, *The Prose of Osip Mandelstam,* North Point Press, 1986. The Russian poet (1891-1938) is often evoked by Voélin.

(p. 189) I. Dilijan, a forested, reclusive resort in the Tavush Province of Armenia.

(p. 191) III. "(Mount) Ararat," the resting place of Noah's Ark according to the Book of Genesis and an essential symbol for Armenians; the mountain is located in the easternmost extremity of Turkey. "Mount Aragats" (or Aragadz) is a volcano complex with four summits and the highest point in Armenia. Lake Sevan is the largest lake in Armenia.

(p. 193) VI. Gregory of Narek (born ca. 945-951, died ca. 1003-1010), the Armenian monk, poet, philosopher, theologian, and the author of the *Book of Lamentations.*

Y.

(p. 197) This sequence, written between March 2011 and July 2012, has not yet been published as (or in) a book. The author has himself made by hand four copies of a chapbook, one of which is in this translator's possession, and attributed it to a press called "Le Mûrier des larmes" (The Blackberry Bush of Tears). The sequence first appeared, bilingually, in *The Fortnightly Review* (December 5, 2015). The epigraph by Dante (1265-1321) comes from *Vita nuova,* XXIV.

(p. 209) XI. Antoine Watteau (1684-1721), the French painter.

(p. 213) XIII. Frida Kahlo (1907-1954), the Mexican artist.

Voices in the Other Language

(p. 229) **The Squawking Sky.** The epigraph by Johannes Bobrowski (1917-1965) is taken from his poem "Ondine" ["Water sprite"] in *Ce qui vit encore* (Paris: L'Aphée, 1987). In German, this poem can be found in *Wetterzeichen* (Berlin: Union Verlag, 1966).

(p. 229) "In my song the sovereign grass / the high grass across the fields—the grass / rising around the skulls—how neglectful / covering just the long bones." The imagery suggests a battlefield with corpses, and Voélin has associated this poem with the genocide in Rwanda and the Yugoslav Wars. One also thinks of his poem *The Poem in Armenia*, which uses as its epigraph similar lines from Osip Mandelstam's *Journey to Armenia*: "I felt like hurrying back to the place where people's skulls are equally beautiful in the grave and at work."

(p. 231) "If You came / with your words—those that go before You." According to the poet, the poem echoes Eugenio Montale's "Sulla colonna più alta (*Moschea di Damasco*)": "Dovrà posarsi lassù / il Cristo giustiziere / per dire la sua parola. / Tra il pietrisco dei sette greti, insieme / s'umilieranno corvi e capinere, / ortiche e girasoli." Jonathan Galassi translates the Italian original as follows: "Christ the Judge, supposedly, / will stand up there / to pronounce his word. / In the rubble of the seven rivers, / crows and blackcaps, nettles and sunflowers, / all will make obeisance together" (*Collected Poems 1920-1954*, New York: Farrar, Straus and Giroux, 1998).

(p. 233) The poem dedicated to Seamus Heaney (1939-2013) commemorates the Irish poet and Nobel prizewinner. Voélin associates the image of suffocating and gasping in this poem, and in the preceding one, with the title of his essay collection, *De l'air volé* (Of Stolen Air, Metis Press, 2011).

(p. 239) "digs into the white shell of millennia." Voélin refers here to the fragmented calcareous soil of his native region and to the shells of the Jurassic period that can be found in freshly plowed fields.

(p. 251) **Voices in the Other Language.** The epigraph by Cristina Campo (1923-1977) is taken from the third section of the poem "Diario byzantino" (1977) in *Entre deux mondes* (Geneva: Ad Solem, 2006). In Italian, this poem can be found in *La tigre assenza* (Milano: Adelphi, 1991).

(p. 251) Christine Lavant (1915-1973), the Austrian poet and artist.

(p. 255) Jean-Bertrand Pontalis (1924-2013), the French writer, editor, and psychoanalyst.

(p. 261) Gerard Manley Hopkins (1844-1889), the Jesuit priest and English poet. The poem alludes to Hopkins' poem "The Wreck of the Deutschland," specifically to the five Franciscan nuns, exiled from Germany, who drowned in the mouth of the Thames when the boat went under. The poem can be found in *The Poems of Gerard Manley Hopkins* (Oxford / New York: Oxford University Press, 4th edition, 1967). See below as well.

(p. 261) "Shipwrecked on stingy England". In French: "Naufragé de la courte Angleterre". Voélin has given me this explanation of the adjective "courte" here, which I have rendered in its sense of insufficiency, narrowness, indeed stinginess: "a metonymy probably, a synecdoche. I was thinking of Victorian England, which was moving quickly into industrialization, and of the spiritual state of the country—of the difficulties of G. M. Hopkins to make himself understood, to his disappointments as a priest. . . that's quite a lot of burden to bear for a simple adjective! The difficult sojourn in Ireland, with G. H. M. haunted by the unknown beauty of God and by human insensitivity, by men 'shut up inside themselves,' too 'courte' in regard to intention, fervor, courage. I was thinking of the conditions of the working class at the time, with no exits available towards the world of thought. I hesitated for a long time about what will remain a judgment, despite the fervor of all those who remain faithful to the Anglican Church or to Newman."

(p. 261) "little tongues of big daisies." Because the botanically precise term "capitula" (for the French "capitules") seemed likely to puzzle the English reader, Voélin suggested that I think of the word, "languettes," which refers to the ordinary petals of a large white daisy. Whence "little tongues" here.

(p. 263) "The hare flees—her leaps through the wind / her claws hardly even— sewing the dry leaves." In regard to this image, Voélin recalls a walk on his birthday in Les Franches Montagnes (in the Jura canton of Switzerland): "Indeed, the female hare's claws just had the time to jab through the leaves, not really enough time to sew them. . . It's the memory of having heard a hare bolting off behind me, and of having watched it going along the edge of the woods in front of me, while making sudden noises on the dry leaves at the end of winter."

(p. 265) Osip Mandelstam (1891-1938), the aforementioned the Russian poet.

(p. 265) The poem dedicated to Nadezhda Mandelstam (1899-1980) was first published by Voélin in *Lents passages de l'ombre* (Castella: Albeuve, 1986). Voélin notes, in his "Glosses" for that book, that the poem "represents the poem-source of the various dedicatory gestures of the collection." He adds that he is "happy . . . to place the poem as a mirror image of the [previous] poem evoking the towering figure of [Nadezhda's] companion of poverty and misfortune, of life, and especially of revolt, the great Russian poet Osip Mandelstam."

(p. 267) Anna Akhmatova (1889-1966), the Russian poet.

(p. 269) The poem dedicated to Emily Dickinson (1830-1886) includes a phrase in italics. Voélin slightly modifies this quotation, which derives from a letter written by the American poet to T. W. Higginson, probably in February 1876, and beginning: "There is so much that is tenderly profane even in the sacredest Human Life—that perhaps it is instinct and not design, that dissuades us from it." The genuine phrase is: "Candor—My Preceptor—is the only wile" (*The Letters of Emily Dickinson*, edited by T. H. Johnson and Theodora Ward, Cambridge, Massachusetts: Harvard University Press, 1986). With respect to this poem, Voélin has evoked the many small children who died during that period of history and adds that he imagines the "plaid blanket" as a sort of "shroud." The last image, "among the scree of eternity," refers, as in a previous poem mentioned above, to the fragmented calcareous soil, with its scree and Jurassic shells, of Voélin's native region.

(p. 271) Elisabeth Bishop (1911-1979), the American poet.

(p. 277) The poem dedicated to "France A." was written, according to Voélin, "to accompany a girl during the year 2014, during the ordeal of her illness and painful stay in the solitude of a hospital."

(p. 283) "Barely an image—on the cross—life / this life from which to make a single one / simple—ordinary." The "cross" here is indeed the cross of Christ, and represents sacrificed life, tortured life. See Voélin's text "Le dieu quelconque" (The Ordinary God), published in the review *La Vouivre: Culture et pensée jungienne* ("Divinités d'Aujourd'hui," No. 14, 2004); that is, "the Son of Man who intended to be an ordinary man, the most ordinary of us all."

(p. 285) Franz Kafka (1883-1924), the German-language writer from Prague, the town with "a hundred church towers," as the saying goes. The line "with the cathedral bells you'll awake" also refers to the bells of the cathedral about 150 meters from Voélin's bedroom window in Fribourg.

(p. 289) "Two sundials". This poem evokes a site from the poet's childhood, the eighteenth-century Garden of the Jesuits, in Porrentruy, which today is a botanical garden. Before entering it, one comes across a Foucault pendulum in a courtyard. Foucault's pendulum offered (in 1851) the first proof of the rotation of the earth.

(p. 289) "pensive pansies." In French, simply "pensées," but the word "pensée" means both "pansy" and "thought." "Pensive pansies" because the flowers are brooding over the demise of love.

(p. 291) **Last Folds of the Promise.** The epigraph by the aforementioned Gerard Manley Hopkins is found in *Poèmes 1876-1889* (Paris: Aubier-Montaigne, 1980). The entire poem, "The Blessed Virgin Compared to the Air We Breathe," can be found in English in *The Poems of Gerard Manley Hopkins* (Oxford / New York: Oxford University Press, 4th edition, 1967).

(p. 297) "Heavily rises the muffle of night." Voélin elucidates this line as follows: "A childhood fascination: cows and their enormous mouths, their nostrils, and their tongues lapping up water from the wooden trough, quenching their thirst before crossing the threshold of the stable—while I was sheltered behind the wire fence of the garden, yet only about fifty centimeters from the muffles, and dumbfounded by their powerful capacity to absorb water, an incredible image of felicitous animal life!"

(p. 299) The poem dedicated to "Grazia B.-R." pays tribute to the poet's Italian translator, Grazia Bernasconi-Romano, who translated *On Brief Death as Sulla morte breve* (Lugano / Milano: Giampiero Casagrande editore, 2006).

(p. 303) "The limping". This poem, written after the disappearance of the poet's mother, during the last days of December 2009, first appeared in a shorter version in *4433: Anthologie du sonnet contemporain* (Geneva: Le Miel de l'Ours, 2012). The "limping" here refers to irregular heartbeats.

(p. 307) Umberto Saba (1883-1957), the Italian poet.

(p. 309) "The unsurpassable Love / that unites the light and the wind." This last line creates an arresting echo with the last line of Dante's *Paradiso*: "L'Amor che move il sole e l'altre stele." "The love that moves the sun and the other stars."

BIBLIOGRAPHY

Poetry

Lierres, Fribourg: Le feu de nuict, 1984.

Sur la mort brève / La Nuit osseuse, Albeuve: Castella, 1984.

Lents passages de l'ombre, Albeuve: Castella, 1986.

Les bois calmés, Geneva: La Dogana, 1989.

Parole et famine, Lausanne: Empreintes, 1995.

D'un nœud d'abeilles, Losne: Thierry Bouchard, 1995.

La lumière et d'autres pas, Geneva: La Dogana, 1997.

Sur la mort brève / La nuit osseuse, Lausanne: Empreintes (Poche Poésie paperback edition, No. 10), 1999.

Dans l'œil millénaire, Le Chambon-sur-Lignon: Cheyne éditeur, 2005.

L'été sans visage, Lausanne: Empreintes, 2010.

Des voix dans l'autre langue, Geneva: La Dogana, 2015

De l'enfance éperdue, Saint-Clément-de-Rivière: Fata Morgana, 2017

Essays

La nuit accoutumée, Geneva: Zoé, 2002.

De l'air volé, Geneva: MétisPresses, 2012.

Other noteworthy essays:

Hommage à Ossip Mandelstam, Fribourg, Limited edition with an engraving by Dominique Lévy, 1986.

"Sur deux nappes de silence," in *Arts poétiques* (anthology), Geneva: La Dogana, 1996.

"Les mots génocidés" in *Les mots du génocide* (anthology), Geneva: MétisPresses, 2012.

Translations into foreign languages (books and anthologies)

Una antologia dela poesia Suiza francesca contenporanea, translated into Spanish, Barcelona: El Bardo, 1985.

Anthologie de la poésie suisse romande, translated into Arabic by Ahmad Al Dosari, Egypt, 2003.

Sulla morte breve, translated into Italian by Grazia Bernasconi-Romano, Lugano / Milano: Gianpiero Casagrande, 2006.

Das verborgene Licht der Jarhreszeiten (anthology), edited and translated into German by Hans Thill, Heidelberg: Das Wunderhorn, 2007.

Die Lyrik der Romandie, edited by Philippe Jaccottet, translated into German by Elisabeth Edl and Wolfgang Matz, Munich: Nagel & Kimche, 2008.

New European Poets, edited by Wayne Miller and Kevin Prufer, poems by Voélin translated into English by Ellen Hinsey, St Paul: Graywolf Press, 2008.

Modern and Contemporary Swiss Poetry, edited by Luzius Keller, poems by Voélin translated into English by John Taylor, Victoria, Texas / London / Dublin: Dalkey Archive Press, 2012.

Poetas suizos: Pierre Voélin, selected poems translated into Spanish by Mario Camelo, Auroraboreal, 2016.

Translations into foreign languages (journals, reviews, literary websites)

Into English: *The Bogman's Cannon* (May 2015), *The Bitter Oleander* (Volume 21, No. 2, Fall 2015; and Volume 23, No. 1, Spring 2017),*The Fortnightly Review* (December 2015), *Samgha* (December 2015).

Into Polish: *Poezja ze Szwajcarii (Poésie de la Suisse)* in *Nowa okolica poetów,* Okolica szwajcarska, no 21, Rzeszòv, 2/2006

THE BITTER OLEANDER PRESS
LIBRARY OF POETRY

TRANSLATION SERIES

Torn Apart / Déchirures by Joyce Mansour
—translated from the French by Serge Gavronsky
Children of the Quadrilateral by Benjamin Péret
—translated from the French by Jane Barnard and Albert Frank Moritz
Edible Amazonia by Nicomedes Suárez-Araúz
—translated from the Spanish by Steven Ford Brown
A Cage of Transparent Words by Alberto Blanco
—translated from the Spanish by Judith Infante, Joan Lindgren,
Elise Miller, Edgardo Moctezuma, Gustavo V. Segade,
Anthony Seidman, John Oliver Simon & Kathleen Snodgrass
Afterglow / Tras el rayo by Alberto Blanco
—translated from the Spanish by Jennifer Rathbun
Of Flies and Monkeys / De singes et de mouches by Jacques Dupin
—translated from the French by John Taylor
1001 Winters / 1001 Tolves by Kristiina Ehin
—translated from the Estonian by Ilmar Lehtpere
Tobacco Dogs / Perros de tabaco by Ana Minga
—translated from the Spanish by Alexis Levitin
Sheds / Hangars by José-Flore Tappy *
—translated from the French by John Taylor
Puppets in the Wind by Karl Krolow
—translated from the German by Stuart Friebert
Movement Through the End / Mouvement par la fin by Philippe Rahmy
—translated from the French by Rosemary Lloyd
Ripened Wheat / 熟了麦子 Selected poems of Hai Zi / 海子 **
—translated from the Chinese by Ye Chun
Confetti-Ash: Selected Poems of Salvador Novo
—translated from the Spanish by Anthony Seidman & David Shook
Territory of Dawn: Selected Poems of Eunice Odio
—translated from the Spanish by Keith Ekiss, Sonia P. Ticas & Mauricio Espinoza
The Hunchbacks' Bus / Autobuzul cu cocoșați by Nora Iuga
—translated from the Romanian by Adam J. Sorkin & Diana Manole
To Each Unfolding Leaf Selected Poems of Pierre Voélin (1976-2015)
—translated from the French by John Taylor

* Finalist for National Translation Award from American Literary Translators Association—2015
** Finalist for Lucien Stryk Asian Translation Award from American Literary Translators Association—2016

THE BITTER OLEANDER PRESS LIBRARY OF POETRY

ORIGINAL POETRY SERIES

The Moon Rises in the Rattlesnake's Mouth by Silvia Scheibli

On Carbon-Dating Hunger by Anthony Seidman

Where Thirsts Intersect by Anthony Seidman

Festival of Stone by Steve Barfield

Infinite Days by Alan Britt

Vermilion by Alan Britt

Teaching Bones to Fly by Christine Boyka Kluge

Stirring the Mirror by Christine Boyka Kluge

Travel Over Water by Ye Chun

Gold Carp Jack Fruit Mirrors by George Kalamaras

Van Gogh in Poems by Carol Dine

Giving Way by Shawn Fawson *

If Night is Falling by John Taylor

The First Decade: (1968-1978) by Duane Locke

Empire in the Shade of a Grass Blade by Rob Cook

Painting the Egret's Echo by Patty Dickson Pieczka **[2012]

Parabola Dreams by Alan Britt & Silvia Scheibli

Child Sings in the Womb by Patrick Lawler

The Cave by Tom Holmes** [2013]

Light From a Small Brown Bird by Rich Ives

The Sky's Dustbin by Katherine Sánchez Espano **[2014]

All the Beautiful Dead by Christien Gholson **[2015]

Call Me When You Get to Rosie's by Austin LaGrone **[2016]

*   Utah Book Award Winner (2012)
** Bitter Oleander Press Library of Poetry Award Winners (BOPLOPA)

The font used in this book is the digital representation of a family of type developed by William Caslon (1692-1766). Printer Benjamin Franklin introduced Caslon into the American colonies, where it was used extensively, including the official printing of *The Declaration of Independence* by a Baltimore printer. Caslon's fonts have a variety of design, giving them an uneven, rhythmic texture that adds to their visual interest and appeal. The Caslon foundry continued under his heirs and operated until the 1960s.